THE LOVEBOOK

A JOAN KAHN BOOK

THE
LOVEBOOK

WHAT WORKS IN A LASTING SEXUAL RELATIONSHIP

By PIERRE MORNELL, M.D.

HARPER & ROW, PUBLISHERS
New York, Evanston, San Francisco, London

1817

FIRST EDITION

DESIGNED BY SIDNEY FEINBERG

Library of Congress Cataloging in Publication Data

Mornell, Pierre.
  The lovebook.
  Includes bibliographical references.
  1. Sex in marriage. 2. Interpersonal relations.
I. Title.
HQ10.M673   301.41'8   73–14274
ISBN 0–06–013055–5

For Linda

For a man and wife to live intimately together is not an easy thing at best. If it's not just exactly right in every way it's practically impossible . . .

—Marilyn Monroe

Contents

Acknowledgments

I am indebted to those good friends who read the manuscript and offered numerous helpful suggestions: Alexandra Botwin, Ph.D., Kathy Fregulia, Geraldine Green, Larry Green, Jane Wheelwright, and Joseph Wheelwright, M.D. For her invaluable help, a special thanks to my editor at Harper & Row, Joan Kahn. For her continuing friendship and encouragement, my deepest appreciation to Rhoda Boyd. And, for their kindness beyond the call of duty, the women of the Redwood Book Store in Mill Valley, California, also deserve my fondest thanks.

Each section contains a maximum number of practical examples and minimum amount of theoretical discussion. A ratio largely possible because of individuals who shared with me not only their seas of problems but, also, their islands of success. To these men and women, I am profoundly grateful. Indeed, it is their success upon which I have tried to focus my primary attention.

And finally, to my wife, Linda. No words of dedication could adequately acknowledge her major contribution to every idea and each page that follows. To say the very least, no book would have been possible without her. But more important, her presence over the years has afforded daily proof of how centering is an intimate relationship. On a more personal note, her love has allowed me to see life as it could be lived and to make some kind of sense out of the world.

Introduction: Life After Orgasm

Hundreds of books have been written about the last few minutes in lovemaking. Over recent years, there's been much to do about orgasms: vaginal orgasms, clitoral orgasms, single orgasms, multiple orgasms, simultaneous orgasms, liberated orgasms, premature and nonexistent orgasms.

Such a preoccupation with the climax of intercourse, I believe, misses the point of a good lasting sexual relationship. When trying to achieve intimacy, it is not a six- or sixty-second performance that counts. Stated simply: My own feeling is that when the other twenty-three hours and fifty-nine minutes in a couple's day are gratifying, orgasms tend to take care of themselves. Or, in broader terms: I think that a couple's relationship out of bed cannot be separated from what happens to them in bed.

Most of us know, for example, that daily praise cannot be divorced from nightly affection; levels of fatigue before lights-out from levels of performance afterward; or feelings of closeness and distance from sexual successes and failures. We know that if a couple fails to support each other or resolve arguments lovemaking suffers. As does it when two people can't talk—before bedtime as well as after it. In short, most of us recognize that our twenty-four hours cannot be separated from those twenty-four (plus or minus) minutes of wild or boring sex with the person we love.

Of course, the reverse is also true. With a good sex life, couples are more willing to invest time and energy into their daily relationship. They are better motivated to support each other, talk together, and resolve problems.

They are more open to their sexual feelings and fantasies, before, during, and after lovemaking.

Hence, the purpose of this book is to discuss sex, not as "an island, entire to itself" but as part of a larger relationship. In the next nine chapters there follows a bit of common and uncommon sense about conversation, support, arguments, fantasies, making love, values, practice, roles, and making changes in that relationship.

I have attempted in these chapters to present an optimistic view of lasting intimacy. The "for better" part of marriage. The "what *does* work" side of living together. But here, a word of caution: One assumption throughout all sections is the existence of basic good will between partners. Actually, the book's focus is upon the inner world of two people who enjoy one another's company (most of the time).

Accentuating the positive, I have also tried to avoid vague generalities such as: A sexual role is like watching a ship on the horizon through a patchy fog. Sometimes the outline is clear; sometimes it's clouded. Instead, I have substituted specific words and examples. (On roles for instance: A wife awakes in bed on Sunday morning caught between two realities: her husband's erection and her children's demands. What is the woman's role? What is the man's? Wherein lies her allegiance? Wherein lies his?)

To this end, the late Dr. Haim Ginott's style and format for describing communications between parents and children provided an invaluably helpful model in presenting specific communications between husband and wife.*

* Although sons and daughters are mentioned in numerous examples throughout each chapter, the total impact of children on a couple's relationship is not given direct attention. In fact, I believe that is the proper subject for another book.

Finally, a brief note on the terms "husband and wife," "him and her," "relationship and marriage." I apologize to those readers who are upset with my constant reference to the individual in a sexual relationship as "him." To paraphrase Dr. Spock's original introduction: It's awkward to say "him or her" each time and I needed "her" to refer to the woman. So, too, the use of "wife, husband, and marriage" is not meant to exclude nonmarried readers, male or female. Marriage is simply the context—both professionally and personally—in which I best understand the meaning of intimacy. However, it's my hope that principles outlined in this book will prove helpful to any two people engaged in an ongoing, warm, and loving relationship.

THE LOVEBOOK

Talking: On Speaking Terms

> *On speaking terms:* Having a relationship friendly enough
> to allow for . . . conversation.
> —WEBSTER'S DICTIONARY

One of the most frequent complaints heard from couples enter-
ing my office is that "We don't seem to talk as much these days."
And yet, talking seems to me the very life blood of any close relationship.

Although husbands and wives today are saturated with the
fact that they should "communicate" with each other, the
means of achieving that communication often remain elusive.
Thus, specific patterns of talking (and not talking), which
couples have found helpful in everyday living, become the
subject of this first chapter.

A Nightly Review:
"What Did You Do Today?"

Wringing out the sponge

Between the morning alarm and call to dinner, many of us
spend our day being soaked to the saturation point.

When two people finally sit down at night, I think that it

helps if each person has a chance to squeeze his inner sponge and wring out as much of the day's trivia as time and memory will allow. In reviewing their day—even for fifteen minutes—a husband and wife can be helpful to each other in two ways: By sharing his news, one person unwinds. And, by listening, the other person keeps his finger on the daily pulse.

Before describing these benefits in more detail, let me mention a frequent first question asked by many couples when I suggest this review. Some ask: "How can we share our day at night, when we live in such different worlds from eight to five? We speak a foreign language." For example: What do a mechanic and his wife review about crankshafts and pistons? How does a psychiatric nurse talk about schizophrenia with her salesman husband? How does a dentist translate the boring details of root canals to his wife? Or a lawyer share his client's confidences with anyone?

While it is true that most jobs do involve a bit of technical jargon, our daily life also includes a language we all understand. We can review the tortures of commuting: catching or missing the 8:11 and 5:17, traffic conditions and weather reports, plans to move closer or change jobs. We can review not only projects and people at work, but the politics necessary to win friends and influence promotions. We can review the pleasure of lunch with friends, walks in the park, afternoons off, or thoughts about a three-day weekend. We can review feelings, not only of blues, boredom, and restlessness, but also feelings of an occasional job well done. And, on very rare days, of everything going right.

If a wife stays home, she lives a more predictable routine. Her life includes the monotony of household chores: morning dishes, marketing, cleaning, cooking, and the rising cost of everything. Yet she can briefly review that routine. She can review being saturated with children and car pools, appointments and arrangements, phone calls and phone bills. She can review the relief that comes with favorite projects: baking, gardening, sewing, getting out of the house. And she can review those comings and goings outside the home—from volunteering services to attending courses to meetings with friends and acquaintances.

Our news may seem trivial. Indeed, it may be monotonous or foolish, except to the person we love. Involved with our trials and tribulations, he is the logical person to absorb the daily overflow from our reservoir of misadventures. But the fact is: *We need to talk.* And if our husband or wife won't listen to us, who will? (Someone who understands? Our secretary? The boss? The girls? Or boys? A bartender? A shrink?)

When we share the minor intimate details of our daily preoccupations, such preoccupations tend to intrude less into the evening hours. After we unwind, it is easier for us to listen. In squeezing our inner sponge, we not only relax but we are again ready to be refilled, alone or together. And the resulting climate at home is more favorable for better listening and better conversation.

A finger on the pulse

Husbands and wives benefit from this nightly review in the role of listener, simply by keeping in touch with the other person. After public demands are reviewed and shared, it becomes much easier for couples to coordinate and meet each other's private demands.

For example: Let's say that a man returns from a trip to Hawaii. He has interviewed for a job and is offered the position. Working late the next three nights, he discusses the trip with several associates, but not with his wife. On the fourth day, understandably, she asks the results of his interviews. And there ensues the following exchange:

Wife: Do you realize that I have yet to hear about the trip?

Husband: Sorry, darling. It's been a three-ring circus at work.

Wife: Will I hear the details before you forget them?

Husband: Let's talk on Sunday. I have meetings every night this week.

Wife: Before Sunday! Are we moving to Hawaii?

Husband: It's the chance of a lifetime. But it all depends on your reaction.

On Sunday, the wife's reaction is to give her husband a hard time about changing jobs in mid-career.

When couples don't involve one another in new plans, the person left in the dark often reacts negatively to those plans. In this case, the wife actually took several months to make an honest decision. Not included in the planning or complexities of the question, how could she intelligently participate in its answer? Before and after the trip, it would have proved helpful if the husband had realized: "My wife needs to hear both advantages and disadvantages of uprooting the family—not only from me, but from women who have lived in the islands. In a sense, we need our own night meetings."

In the business of making and reporting daily news, there should be no silent partners. If two people feel included, their understanding and helpfulness increase, and a couple's base of nightly conversation is broadened to encompass both of their worlds. "What did you do today" need only be the first line of an opening fifteen-minute review. Major productions can come later.

Listening:
The Key to Talking

We all know the experience of talking with a friend, parent, teacher, or doctor who listens to us without rushing us. Such a person helps us to relax as well as helps our conversation to flow. Yet, the experience of talking with a good listener is a surprisingly rare one.

The fact is that listening requires energy. It may seem easy, but it takes concentration and patience. It is a process that is active, not passive. The person who listens well is clearly more than "a born listener." Knowingly or unknowingly, he must work at it. And good conversation ultimately hinges upon such silent efforts because, quite obviously, meaningful talk—like meaningful sex—involves two people.

However, there are times when a well-intentioned person cannot listen. Even with the best equipment, static will frequently jam his airways. The interference may originate between one's ears: such as from inner fatigue, anger, or preoccupations with other problems. While, in other cases, the source of trouble is more obvious: radios, record players, television sets, or the rising decibels of a children's chorus. This roar from the crowd or racket in our head is a fact of life. And, should the noise level become ear-splitting, a person will concede: "Sorry, I can't talk now."

But, in spite of this reality, most people feel that they should be able to *listen* whenever their partner begins to talk. They have not learned to say that the message being received is weak and the fault lies with their own antennae.

Maybe couples need permission to tell each other not only: "I can't talk now," but also: "Sorry, love, I can't listen now." An announcement which leads directly to the crucial matter of silence, quiet time, and the need for privacy in every good ongoing sexual relationship. In short: It leads us to the need for couples not to talk with each other in marriage.

Quiet Time: The Need for Privacy

Early in a relationship, I think that many couples find silence to be uncomfortable. If one partner lapses into silence, the other partner often interprets the quiet as synonymous with boredom or anger or disapproval. He takes it personally. Consequently, many people are surprised—and relieved—to hear that silence is a necessity for survival in any intimacy between husband and wife.

There is a vignette about an eighteen-year-old college freshman who was relatively nervous before his first weekend of camping with a new girl friend. The boy asked a favorite uncle, in whom he confided, "Unk, what am I going to talk with her about for two straight days?" To which his uncle roared back: "My God! I haven't the foggiest idea—it sounds exhausting!"

Later, the uncle suggested that his nephew and girl friend spend *at least* two hours alone on both days. Until he returned on Sunday night, the lad didn't really understand this advice. However, exhausted and exhilarated by a successful two days, the boy thanked his uncle for his advice to take a time out for silence. His conclusion: "Frankly, we couldn't have lasted the weekend without it."

After months or years of living together, many couples are struck by a fundamental reality: They love a person, yet they want to leave him (at least, temporarily). Some people become immobilized on the horns of this dilemma. The following incident is not untypical.

Six months after her marriage, a wife who was a social worker began to spend increasing amounts of time behind a locked door in the bathroom. Her husband, an architect, was predictably confused and upset by his wife's closed-door policy. He saw it as a dramatic change from her premarital behavior, about which, however, he had relatively little first-hand knowledge. (Because they had lived five hundred miles apart before marriage, the couple had fallen in love via long distance. Their living together was limited to a few intense weekends, and both kept telling each other they dreamt of the time when "We'll never be separated.")

Separation, of course, was to become their problem. In a

later session with her best girl friend, the wife confided: "He wants me with him every minute—it's unbelievable. The only time I can be alone is in the bathroom. Not only is it a nuisance, but I'm going crazy."

Here, an intelligent couple did not recognize their obvious but opposite needs. At the end of her day, the wife was drained by her intense contact with people at work. She came home and craved a quiet period. The husband, however, spent his eight hours over an architect's drawing board. By evening, he was starved to talk. The outcome of this couple's collision course was the wife's detour into the bathroom—which proved not only perplexing for the husband, but uncomfortable for the wife. Let us ask at this point: Were there alternatives? And if so, what actions might have been more direct and more effective?

After coming home, the wife could have declared a moratorium. Before dinner her husband might have read the paper or puttered around while she was quiet in another room. Or, he might have left for a half-hour's walk, allowing his wife the luxury of being alone in the house. They might have talked before supper—or during it—and then adjourned for individual activity for the evening's duration.

Any combination of these styles might have provided this couple with a rhythm of coming together and moving away, of participation and privacy. With this vital and necessary balance, they may have soon discovered that peaceful coexistence was possible within the same house, as well as the same room.

The desire for privacy: negative reaction or positive request?

Couples should realize that desires to love and to leave their partner need not be incompatible. That there is a universal feeling in marriage: "I need to get away from you." A feeling often translated into an excuse to leave home: forgotten errands or frequent emergencies, weeknight appointments or weekend arrangements.

This need to escape, however, can also be expressed more directly by a clear and positive statement. For example, if a person can say:

"I'm restless and a drive might help."
"I'd like some quiet time in the bathtub."
"Under a hairdryer, I can sit down and shut out the world."
"Where's my newspaper? I want to hide for twenty minutes."
"A walk sounds good. I want to unwind."
"Let's wait to talk. I'd like an hour to read."

The following sentence can be added: *"I need to fill up."*

This statement allows us to ask for privacy without blaming the other person. It labels the stimulus for silence as coming from our own inner needs.

Specific words aside, my point is simply that, if we find ourselves thinking "I must get out of here," we need not always be reacting to a loved one. Indeed, we are often responding to a very human and magnetic pull. Filling up is the attraction of privacy. To be replenished is the reason to be alone. To relax and come back refreshed is the goal of silence.

This perspective comes with experience and practice. It comes when we listen to our internal warning bells: "I don't want to talk" or "I can't listen." At those points, we can usually say, with some degree of confidence: "Time out. I need to fill up."

Conversations in Public

At times, the correction of small problems can lead to big improvements in how couples talk to each other. Conversation in mixed company is one illustration of this principle.

A friend who worked in Washington, D.C., several years ago described the ritual of one's social life in that capital city. He explained that all of the husbands invited to small dinner parties were more-often-than-not of equal bureaucratic rank or governmental status. (Senators with senators, undersecretaries with undersecretaries, G-14's with G-14's, and so forth.) And the evening routine was always similar: After dessert, cigars were passed to the men, then, following the first puff of smoke, each couple moved in opposite directions and regrouped themselves according to sex. He explained that all wives were expected to disappear for the duration of the evening. Social intercourse was not only segregated, but after-dinner discussion was also channeled into two divisions of shop talk: political gossip for the men and general gossip for the women.

In contrast to this method of entertaining, another friend spoke of an evening party in Paris. She recalled that the passing of brandy and cigars also signaled the end of supper. But on this occasion, couples went together into one small drawing room, where the conversation proved to be absolutely sparkling for everyone. According to our friend: "It was the most brilliant display of verbal fireworks I ever heard."

When our second friend was told of the Washington story, she added a missing punch line about her Parisian night. It summarized one difference between the two evenings. "In America, you said the ladies were their husband's wives. But, in France, of course, they were their mistresses."

The Washington-Paris polarities are admittedly extreme examples. Yet, commonly, for many of us at parties, rather than going in different directions, we find ourselves talking in different directions. How often do we hear in the midst of a single conversation a constant stream of side comments: "If I've heard this story once, I've heard it . . ." Or, "That's news. We never talk at home these days . . ." Or, "How old are your kids now?"

The tendency to talk in opposite directions is a habit of both men and women. A husband is as likely to derail his wife in mid-sentence as is she to interrupt him with questions about the hostess' children. Regardless of who is at fault, however, I believe that this pattern is unhelpful. It causes a pair to overlook the small, but important, opportunity to share the same conversation.

To improve the situation, a couple should first decide if fourway conversations among six close friends are a problem. If so, changes might be considered for any of the following reasons:

1. We can always go in opposite directions at other times and in other places. (For example: at home, alone with friends, or in larger public gatherings.)

2. If we are segregated by sex, our discussion frequently reverts to daily shop talk. Whereas in front of a mixed audience, we often give a more interesting performance.

3. When we listen to our husband or wife in public, their self-respect and self-esteem are increased.

4. When we share the conversation of an evening, our thoughts and feelings can later be exchanged on a common ground. (Rather than going home and saying to one another: "What did you talk about tonight?" "Oh, I don't know. Nothing really—and you?" "Oh nothing." "Well, good night." "Good night.")

(For more discussion of couples functioning together in public: See "Beyond the Anger," page 130.)

Messages in Code:
The Secret Rules

Most of us know that children have fun in creating games with special roles—like, "I'll be a doctor. You're my nurse." In order to play, we also realize that a child must go on to explain the unwritten rules, often in elaborate detail. As most kids have once said to a brother, sister, or playmate: "Let's pretend this bed is our office and no one is here. We have to examine each other and I think that you should go first. Take off your shoes, loosen your belt, unzip your zipper, and hide in that closet if my mom comes home."

Do we, as adults, outgrow this desire to play games with special roles? Not really. We may, however, forget to explain the necessary rules. We neglect to give clues, which could solve hidden mysteries. We often speak a foreign language and don't translate. For example: Two brief scenes in a couple's bedroom:

Scene I: (Night—after lights are out)

He: Pretty tired luv?

She: Mmmmmmmmmmmmmm.

He: Feel like snuggling before we go to sleep?

She: . . . I'm pretty tired . . .

He: (*Rolling over and away*) Okay, good night babe . . .

She: Mmmmmm . . .

Ten minutes later the wife is awake: turning and tossing, up and back to the bathroom.

He: What's wrong?

She: . . . Nothing . . .

He: Come on, something's wrong.

She: No, really, I'm fine. Just forget it and go to sleep.

Scene II: (The next morning)

She: You really hurt me last night.

He: I did? How?

She: You don't have any idea what I'm talking about?

He: Not a clue.

She: Then, there's simply no point in my telling you . . .

He: Don't be ridiculous. If I upset you, I want to know what I did.

She: If you're that insensitive, I don't know where to begin.

He: So tell me.

Here, the wife storms out of the room—leaving her secret and her husband in the dark.

From a wife's point of view, the location of her treasure may be obvious; but she must clearly share a piece of the map with her husband. In this case, after time and distance had passed, the couple might have found the subject easier to discuss. Later that night, the wife might have said:

"Last night I wanted to be seduced. But it should have been your idea."

"If you give up so easily, how can you really want me?"

"There are times I need to feel like Scarlett O'Hara being carried up that long stairway. If I have to tell you, I won't be Scarlett."

"Sometimes words spoil everything. Just look at me and guess what I'm feeling."

"I often say things that I don't mean. It's a silly test. I want to be won."

Such instructions, I think, help to preserve the magic in a marriage. It is only when couples do understand each other's signals, however, that a minimum of words are necessary to continue whatever magic exists between them. Because this matter of signals in bed is so important, I have discussed it in detail in Chapter 5. (See "Breaking the Sound Barrier," page 80 and "Sexual Complaints," page 83.)

Clear Messages:
Risks and Results

Why do most people find it hard to speak clearly about charged subjects? While straight talk may achieve results, a person does risk being hurt or embarrassed in the act of being clearly understood.

"With your mother's next visit, let's set a departure date with her arrival time," is an invitation to sensitivity on both sides of the in-law question.

"I don't like your keeping gifts from old boy friends (husbands or lovers)" is an admission of a painful jealousy about our partner's past history.

"When we're in bed, please make love, not gas" opens the Pandora's box of bad habits . . . among other things.

It is safer, but less clear, when a hidden wish comes as an indirect hint rather than a direct statement. For example: "Let's see a pornographic film" may be the easiest way of saying: "Our sex life is boring; and maybe we'll be turned on by how they do it in Denmark." Such a maneuver is relatively safe. And it spares both partners from being hurt (or, I think, helped) with the underlying reasons for their sexual boredom. The following is one illustration of a woman's taking verbal gambles to achieve her sexual goals.

Mrs. A, who had been married for seven years, was a poor teacher in bed. After making love, she frequently wanted to be kissed on her breasts—only she lacked the nerve to tell her husband. When intercourse was over, the wife would say: "Kiss me, kiss me." But Mr. A, who had exhausted himself in the previous ten minutes and was falling asleep, would kiss Mrs. A on the lips and think: "Kiss her? Kiss her? I am kissing her. Why does she always sound like a broken record?"

One night, Mrs. A, embarrassed all these years to use the word "breasts" or "nipples," mustered the courage to tell her husband. His kissing of her lips quickly shifted to points south.

One problem is that should husband or wife ask for something that is charged or controversial, he or she risks being laughed at for revealing a hidden fantasy. For example, Mrs. A's husband might have responded:

"Kiss your breasts?! Why now?"
"Have you been reading one of those sex books?"
"But I want to sleep after we make love . . ."

Or worse, he might have said (and done) nothing.

Of course, Mrs. A might have elected to remain silent and speak with actions rather than words. A small move of her husband's head to the right spot might have accomplished the same purpose. In either communication, however, the meaning of "Kiss me, kiss me" becomes obvious rather than being obscure. And a closed secret becomes an open subject in relatively painless fashion.

My feeling is that it's seldom possible to take shortcuts in charged areas. To speak clearly is to take risks and be vulnerable —whether the forbidden topic is sex, in-laws, money, religion, past history, irritating habits, or whatever. Maybe it is using a foghorn when a whisper would do in summarizing the conclusion: To achieve intimacy, two people must discover ways to exchange feelings, expose fantasies, and express ideas without fear of laughter or humiliation from the person they love.

The Common Ground

In order for couples to talk, there must be something to talk about. When husband and wife work all day in separate worlds, they need to find a common ground of mutual interests beyond a fifteen-minute review of daily routines. In contrast, two people engaged in similar activities or working together are luckier— their outside life is a daily springboard to nightly conversation. In both instances, however, I feel that there is more to meaningful conversation than meets the eye.

Officially, most people enjoy a wide range of shared experiences. They talk about sports, television, movies, books, restaurants, plays, news, music, hobbies, clothes, cars, politics, and so forth. Such common ground is important and is easily identified. It is the focus of conversation with acquaintances and friends . . . and each other.

Unofficially, however, many couples' conversation is something else. It is a far cry from television or films, clothes or automobiles, sports or current events. It transcends all of them and is the true basis of an intimate relationship. This unofficial common ground is not unlike the bottom of an iceberg. It is the largest part and often remains hidden to the outside world.

What do I mean?

In the privacy of a marriage—on Sunday drives or dinners alone—our talk is filled with small words and half-broken sentences. Our peculiar language is so cryptic, so coded, so terribly scrambled that most of us can't recall our conversations from one night to the next morning. It is everything that comes together at once—spoken and unspoken, future and past, trivial and mundane, dreams and reality—all that is highly irrelevant, except to two people in love, who can spend hours upon hours talking between the lines.

Describing this private world as viewed by an outsider, Edwin O'Conner captured it eloquently in *The Edge of Sadness* when he wrote:*

They talked some more; once again I saw that I had arrived at the border of the unknown land: the private preserve of husband and wife. Over the years I must have come to this precise spot literally a hundred times . . . and yet each time it never fails to jolt me a little, I imagine it's the sheer swiftness of the passage, for one thing: it always happens in an instant. One moment you may be talking to an old friend, someone you've known so well you would have sworn there is very little left to know, and then suddenly that someone will turn and speak to someone else in an entirely different way: a way so special, so direct and intimate that you wonder why words were used at all—it's as if the two had met head on and fused some-

* Edwin O'Conner, *The Edge of Sadness* (Boston, Little, Brown, 1961)

where in mid-air before a syllable was spoken. And this is the point at which you realize that the old friend you know so well has in fact dimensions you will never know—just as you realize this way of speaking, this kind of encounter which is so personal, so completely *shared*, is also something you will never know. Which is really no great revelation, you may have realized all this often enough before, but, as I say, each fresh recognition brings its own jolt home. Unless you are careful—and sometimes even then—it is a sentimental moment . . ."

2

Being Supportive: United We Stand, Divided We Fall

Support: To give courage, faith, or confidence to; help; comfort; strengthen. To give approval to; be in favor of; subscribe to; sanction; uphold.

—WEBSTER'S DICTIONARY

The Call Light Above Room 409

The following story emphasizes the necessity of paying attention when things go well in any relationship. It is an incident I often mention to couples in my office who report responding to each other primarily from crisis to crisis.

These events happened at the University of California Medical Center in 1966. As a second-year psychiatric resident, I was called by the head nurse on a surgical floor whose staff refused to answer the call light above room 409. "We're having trouble with a forty-three-year-old woman recovering from gall-bladder surgery," the nurse began. "Her name is Mrs. P, and she was operated on last Thursday. Her first postoperative day, Friday, she didn't complain and we hardly noticed her. Mrs. P was the model patient—or so we thought before the weekend. I was off Saturday and Sunday, but on Monday the morning report was unanimous: Our 'model gall bladder in 409' had become a 'monstrous pain-in-the-ass.'

"Apparently on Saturday, Mrs. P changed. She turned on her call light and wouldn't switch it off. Her demands were fired off like machine guns: pain pills, laxatives, bed pan, magazines, extra pillows, adjust her window, check the I.V. You name it. On every eight-hour shift, the orderlies and nurses were spending eighty percent of their time in 409. By Sunday morning, the staff was exhausted. Today, even the interns are furious, and avoid the woman as if she had the plague."

In reviewing the case: On Friday the patient had done well and wasn't seen. Over the weekend, room 409 had been entered dozens of times, but only when the call light went *on*. In effect, Mrs. P talked with the staff only when she had a complaint. As the woman continued to make demands out of all proportion to her physical condition, it was natural to assume that she was asking for more than laxatives and bed pans. But what did she want?

To find out, a minor shift in tactics was discussed and within forty-eight hours the crisis ended.

It was decided that Mrs. P was to be given more attention— but only when she was calm and quiet. Whenever 409's light went *off,* a nurse was assigned to enter the patient's room and visit with her for ten or fifteen minutes. The same nurse was told to give this kind of attention several times a day, but never when the light was on. Over Tuesday and Wednesday, "the gall bladder in 409" demanded less and talked more. Discussion between nurse and patient went well beyond cathartics or codeine. By Thursday morning, Mrs. P's call light went off for the last time. Having a chance to tell her story, the patient finally relaxed. And so did the staff.

In retrospect, the solution was obvious. It turned out the woman was terrified. For weeks before surgery, she was worried her doctor wasn't telling the complete truth. With a family history of malignancy, Mrs. P was convinced her attacks of colic were the early pains of cancer. But she was a "good patient" and afraid to "bother" the surgeon. However, after the operation, (naturally) there was no mention of cancer. So her fears persisted. On Friday she had tried to see the doctor alone and question him, but his rounds were hurried. Consequently, she felt embarrassed and remained the model patient.

With the result: The nursing staff almost forgot her. By Saturday, however, the woman's fear turned to panic. Finding the call light, Mrs. P soon became locked into a vicious cycle of self-defeating behavior with the nurses. Behavior that continued until common sense prevailed.

Paying attention between crises

On an individual basis: The difficulties inherent in paying attention between call lights or crises can also be demonstrated during periods of illness and health. For instance, most of us have shared the following experience.

We take our body for granted until it hurts. Yet, when illness occurs, we quickly and naturally focus on that part of our anatomy which causes pain. Our energy is consumed by discomfort. A throbbing sinus, stuffed nose, tense stomach, painful back. . . . At such times, we inevitably say to ourselves: "When I'm better, I won't forget. I'll be thankful for every trouble-free day. From now on, I'll be aware of my good health." But as the symptoms pass, we do forget. We find ourselves returning to the daily problems and preoccupations of fighting clocks, answering phones, worrying about weight, paying bills, and doing our best to make ends meet. Thus, in health as in sickness, our daily attention becomes focused on whatever goes wrong. And, in the process, we tend to forget when things go right. So too, I think, do we forget in our relationship with one another.

Hence, the purpose of this chapter is to suggest basic ways that two people might support each other between as well as during the call lights and problems of everyday living.

Praise: The Minimum
Daily Requirement

Can an individual ever hear too much praise? Can a pair ever
offer each other too many *deserved* compliments? Can husbands
and wives ever get "enough" support from the person they love?
Here, let us examine a common experience for many couples—
before and after marriage.

Before marriage, a man courts a woman with daily praise for
how she pleases him. He compliments her on what she does
well. He reflects an image of his lover's better half—seeing life
as it could be, not necessarily as it is. The thoughts of a man in
love are optimistic and open-hearted. His words, especially those
whispered during or after lovemaking, have a way of making his
woman feel supremely important . . . as do her words to him. In
short, during most courtships, two lovers give each other infinite
pleasure by their natural, if rare, habit of accentuating the positive.

After living together for several years, however, life changes.
Two people begin to respond mainly to those call lights and
crises. Daily problems attract more attention than daily solutions.
Instead of praise for good behavior, complaints or silences greet
periods of calm between storms. For a husband and wife to pay
attention to routine good deeds (like paying attention to routine
good health) is more easily said than done. For example: Daily
praise is frequently missing when husband and wife greet each
other at day's end. Silence, where a compliment would do, often
begins the nightly routine and precipitates the justified reaction:
"No one appreciates me."

Let us take the caricature of a husband arriving home with the
familiar announcement: "Wow, it's been one helluva day."

His wife, armed with a newspaper and cold beer, adds a kiss
before returning to her cooking. At dinner the husband eats with

silent enthusiasm. It is only midway through dessert that he un-loads a few burdens of the day and asks his first question of the night: "Hey honey, is there a decent talk show on the idiot box tonight?" The scene ends, not untypically, with the husband fall-ing asleep on the couch in front of television, while his wife goes off to bed.

What are the simplest alternatives to this particular routine?

Little harm would come and positive good might definitely result if the husband could start the evening with something as simple as: "It's good to be home." Or, if that isn't a comfortable statement, he might find a variety of causes under which to fly the banner: "You're special." Such as:

"Did I need a drink tonight. Thanks, love."
"Boy, what a frantic day. Sorry I couldn't call."
"Honey, the house looks nice."
"Honey, you look nice."
      or later:
"What a dinner—you've done it again."
"I've rattled on about my day, how was yours?"

It is true that such expressions may sound like corny clichés. Yet, for those of us who feel dumb or foolish in singing and re-peating our loved one's praises on a daily basis, we need only think how good it feels when such compliments are aimed in our direction. As recipients of praise: Do *we* ever feel foolish in hearing variations on the theme: "You're wonderful . . . special terrific . . ."?

Clichés aside, I believe that there is no substitute for daily compliments to convey the basic message: Our efforts have been noticed and we're appreciated as well as loved. As such, praise becomes the applause we need to rehearse and improve our everyday performances. Or, putting it another way: In order to develop our talents—or when we move from areas of confidence to areas of insecurity—we need all the support we can get. Be it in making dinner or making love, we want to know whenever we're doing a good job. And, therefore, we also need to be told about it.

For example: When a man is too rough in bed, his wife may react critically: "Don't be in such a hurry, darling. You're hurting me." But the wife's complaints about being hurt also hurt. Indeed, sexual criticism, regardless of how mild, will usually trigger a variety of reactions within most men. Such as:

Defensive: "Other women never complained."

Childish: "That's the last time for you."

Confused: "It was good enough for Sunday morning. What's wrong with Tuesday night?"

All of these feelings are understandable but unhelpful. Should the husband want to please his wife, he must put aside these initial responses and try harder to go slower and be more gentle during lovemaking. But when he does improve, the husband needs to know it. No purpose is served by rewarding his more successful efforts with silence.

In other words: Should a man be tender between the sheets, it helps when his wife tells him in the simplest way:

"I loved your being gentle with me,"
    or
"That's exactly what I needed tonight,"
    or
"There are no words . . ."

(Again, for more examples: See "Breaking the Sound Barrier" and "Sexual Complaints" in Chapter 5.)

Such praise—when it is deserved—insures that a delightful and meaningful act doesn't go unnoticed. Before or after dark, compliments become the stimulus necessary for a person to repeat similar behavior and improve upon it. However, I think that praise need not be limited by the borders of a mattress or boundaries of one's own home. In fact, one of the most touching ways to receive a compliment comes after visits to friends, family, or acquaintances. Such meetings often result in the passing on of kind words to a husband about his wife, or vice versa. To share these comments later at home not only comes as a pleasant surprise. But also, it costs only the price of remembering:

> "He was still raving about your dinner of last week."
> "She told me that your sense of humor saved the evening."
> "They asked what a nice person like you was doing with someone like me."
> "She said that I didn't deserve you. I argued."

Such comments, I think, can only result in the husband or wife being left with good feelings about himself as well as the family member, friend, or neighbor who paid the compliment in the first place.

The opposite of bringing compliments home is taking your praise elsewhere. More specifically in public: For example, should the host or hostess at a dinner party greet the husband of a visiting couple with words to the effect: "I've never seen you looking better," and if the man receiving the compliment answers: "Well, it's because I have such a great wife," the conversation stops. Or, people laugh in embarrassment. The husband's spontaneous confession is a shock to everyone within hearing distance. Why a shock? Because the deflection of a compliment aimed at oneself in another's direction is such a rare and thoughtful feat. What is there left to say?

In front of other people it takes skill and sensitivity to drop an appropriate, if infrequent, "You're special." Yet, when it succeeds, the pleasure to the other person is magnified and enjoyed well beyond the one sentence or single evening. Praise, stated with discretion in public, becomes a truly priceless gift which cannot be duplicated.

A final word about praise. In this brief section I have deliberately simplified a complicated issue. Quite obviously, the roots

of an individual's self-confidence and self-esteem can be traced
to his early childhood. A positive view of himself starts with
praise from his parents, teachers, and friends. The quality of that
praise (or lack of it) remains a lifelong influence upon any person's ability to give as well as receive compliments.

But the fact remains: A woman can help her man feel valuable and loved with continued support in their ongoing relationship. As can the man, in similar ways, help his wife to feel
worthwhile and special in the pursuit of her goals. For both, I
think, external substitutes (like the size of one's car or house—
indeed, the size of one's breasts or penis or even paycheck) become less important when each partner knows that his daily es-
teem is validated from an original source. From the person who
loves him most and who knows him best.

Actions and Deeds

When one person wants to support the other person, small nonverbal expressions of his feelings can prove most helpful. In fact,
it is often more rewarding when two people display concern, understanding, sympathy, or appreciation without words. For instance, on the husband's side: Midst an argument, the man
might normally withdraw into silence as his wife bursts into
tears. On the one hand, he might be silently furious and think:

"Oh, my God, not again."
"Whatever I do—it's never enough."
"There goes another evening shot to hell."
"It's time to punt."

On the other hand, he might also feel helpless:

"I really don't know what to say."
"No words would be helpful at this point."
"There's nothing I can do . . . "

Yet, there is something he can do. Rather than remaining
silent or shouting at his wife: "Goddamnit, stop crying and tell

me what's wrong . . . ," he can walk over, take her in his arms, absorb a few tears, and cancel the lecture on hysterics. In short, he can act instead of going on-and-on with either silence or words . . . words . . . words.

Other actions: A man can surprise his wife by bringing flowers on birthdays, anniversaries, or out-of-the-blue. Every day, he can call her at work or home—but to touch base as much as to talk. At day's end, he can act to quiet a hectic house—for example, he can wash dishes rather than complain about them. Or, seeing his wife about to scream, a husband can move his tribe of shrieking Indians out of the house and into a park—making news instead of reporting it.

My point is simply that there comes a time, for wives as well as husbands, to support the person they love by acting and doing . . . in addition to talking.

Asking for Support

When problems are obvious

Support is easiest to give when the person who needs it can say: "Look, I'm hurting . . . and here's the reason . . . "

What is obvious to us, however, is not always clear to other people. So, when our loved one looks blank as we turn pale, I think that we can best get the support we need by:

1. Describing the problem. (As we see it.)
2. Offering a potential solution.

For example: From the wife's viewpoint, specific instances of "Look, I'm hurting and here's what you can do about it" might include:

"I've argued with people all day and can't face another word. What I need tonight is some peace and quiet. Could you answer the phones and censor my calls?"

"My menstrual period is about to start. I feel jittery and on edge—
like I can't cope with things. It should pass by tomorrow; but
tonight, why don't we go out to dinner?"

"When I'm bitchy with you, don't say: 'What is this poison?' or
'Boy, are you on the rag!' Just tell me that it's awful and that you
understand."

"When guests come for dinner, I spend hours cooking. It's rare
when anyone comments on a meal, except to say: 'Thanks for a
lovely evening.' I never know if dinner has been a success or disaster. Why don't you start keeping me posted in the kitchen; or by
squeezing my knee under the table?"

Of course, one problem is that not all our needs for support can
be so clearly recognized and simply stated.

When problems are obscure

If requests for supportive first-aid are the treatment of choice
in obvious injuries, they are also helpful in the more obscure
nicks and scratches of everyday living.

A friend and his wife tell the story of going to his parents'
home the first Christmas vacation after their marriage. He was
relatively calm and relaxed, but his wife was unusually nervous,
as it was the initial extended visit for both generations. On
Christmas morning the wife presented her new mother with six
red candles, which she had made and dipped by hand. The present was received with thanks; but, it wasn't reopened for the
duration of the visit. Each night, the mother would place two
candles on the dinner table. However, these two were store-
bought . . . and white.

By week's end, the wife felt rejected by the insensitivity of
her mother-in-law. Needless to say, her husband's color and
candle blindness was no help. Finally, on their last night, the
wife broke into tears and told her husband the story. With the
result that one recently married son spent his final vacation

morning in the education of his mother. Subject: The care of homemade candles—and the handling of new daughters bearing gifts.

Asking for support, especially over such a seemingly "trivial" matter, did involve a risk on the wife's part. Risk because she was wary of laughter or amazement greeting her violent reaction over such a petty issue. Or worse, her husband's indifference to the whole business over red and white candles. In this situation, fortunately, her husband did come to her aid, doing his best to support his wife rather than undermine her. He tried to improve the situation rather than aggravate it.

A similar story was told by another couple, Mr. R and Mrs. S, a widow and widower in their mid-sixties. Speaking of living arrangements before their impending marriage, they decided that Mr. R's two-bedroom apartment was to be filled with Mrs. S's antique furniture. His possessions were to be moved into storage.

As Mr. R thought of parting with two oil paintings, favorites of his deceased wife, he realized that he felt like a traitor to her memory. With the wedding's approach, he found himself excessively preoccupied about the paintings. And yet, he was embarrassed by his feelings and reluctant to discuss them.

When Mr. R finally raised the problem, he took the same risk over paintings as did the friend's wife over candles. Without thinking, Mrs. S could have reacted with laughter or amazement, opening wounds instead of closing them. Or, she could understand Mr. R's strong feelings about two pictures and support him, while remaining honest in the situation. For instance, she might have told him.:

"I'm not crazy about them. But it makes no difference. Feelings are more important than things."

"You know I don't like them. So what? If they're special to you, they're important to me. . . . And maybe we should talk about putting up family photographs in the apartment. What do you think?"

"No, they don't match the antique furniture. But I didn't realize what those old paintings meant to you. Of course they stay with us."

While paintings or candles may have symbolic meanings to one person, they often remain a mystery to his partner. These symbols—in oil, wax, or whatever—cannot be understood by the "outsider" until they are explained. Whether the issue is large or small, a couple's receiving mutual support involves more than subtle hints and obscure clues. It involves (and requires), I think, straight talk between two people whenever a small hurt is felt. At times, however, the situation calls for more than "straight talk."

What do I mean?

Which Honesty Is the Best Policy?

From time to time, complete honesty may not always be the best policy. On occasions, our "honest" reactions often resemble a mixture of helpful and unhelpful thoughts and feelings. Consequently, when it comes to supporting the person we love, a crucial question becomes: Which honesty is the best policy? A brief example:

One Thursday night, a wife is ready to make love, but her husband is too tired. Her inner reactions might include:

Honest and unhelpful: "I'm willing—but you're always weak."
"That's it for you."
"Wait until next time!"

Honest, but ???:   "If I were tired, would you let me sleep?"

> "Do you realize that we make love
> *only* on Sundays?"

Honest and helpful: "Fine, but hold me for a minute before you go to sleep."
"Okay, let's make love tomorrow. But
you'll have to initiate it."

I say "helpful" and "unhelpful," because when we are helped, not hurt, in moments of vulnerability, feelings of tenderness and affection for the other person are strengthened. And, when we are protected from attack at these moments, we are more receptive to other levels of honesty at other times.

Shortly before she was married, a young lady—Miss Y—had an accident. On her way to San Francisco General Hospital where her fiancé, Dr. Z, worked as a resident physician, she hit the gas pedal instead of the brake and smashed *his* car into a telephone pole.

Miss Y was understandably shaken by the accident. She immediately phoned Dr. Z in the emergency room and said: "Darling, I'm sorry, but I lost control of your car and hit a pole. Other people weren't involved, but I cut my lip."

When she called, Dr. Z was ending a nonstop twenty-four hours on duty. His immediate reactions to the news were conflicting and confusing. He thought:

"How will I pay for it?"
"How badly is she hurt?"
"There's *always* a crisis before my weekend off!"

His first spoken words were: "How damaged is the car?"

After a brief answer—the front bumper was badly dented—Miss Y told Dr. Z that her lip was bleeding and that she might need some stitches. She gave him a few more details about the cut, which went from her inner gum to the outer skin, before agreeing to come to the emergency room. Dr. Z then arranged for a plastic surgeon to do an immediate evaluation. However, driving to meet Dr. Z and reviewing his words, Miss Y recalled that his first question concerned the car. Impulsively, she drove to another hospital—the University Medical Center—where her bleeding lip was closed with seven stitches.

Details aside, this episode is a familiar one to many of us. Dr. Z's reactions were "honest," but the situation called for a more sensitive kind of honesty. Certain feelings in a crisis are almost always helpful. When Miss Y was down, she was not only upset about the car, but she also reached out for a sympathetic word. She called her future husband to hear a warm and understanding voice say:

"Are you okay?"
"How badly were you hurt?"
"Don't worry, love. Where are you? I'm on the way."

She needed support and reassurance and a chance to talk. Instead, she heard: "Damages to machines are more important than damages to me."

Of course, "Tell me about the car?" is a logical and harmless question. Later, it might have been discussed without leading to hurt feelings. As could the more charged and angry reactions. Indeed, after the crisis had passed, Dr. Z did say:

"You're so damn preoccupied with the wedding, you shouldn't drive. We're lucky it wasn't worse."
"Haven't I asked you not to drive at night without your glasses?"
"Why didn't you emphasize the hole in your bloody lip?"

Dr. Z's reactions of anger, upset, and misgivings were legitimate to express, but not at his fiancée's expense. The "whole truth," however, needn't be shared. For example, Dr. Z's initial thoughts of sarcasm, bitterness, revenge, or childish anger were frankly unhelpful to mention at any time. It was unnecessary for him to say (aloud):

"Why do you always pick the weekends?!"
"You'll never drive that car again."

"Didn't I tell you? Didn't I? Didn't I . . . ? "
"Stupid. Idiot. Dum-dum driver!"

These weapons can be collected in private rather than exhibited in public. Harmless in a locked case, they need not be removed and fired at the people we love. (For more examples, see: "Concern—Kill 'em in Private," page 33.)

To repeat two previous statements: When we are helped not hurt, in moments of vulnerability, feelings of warmth and affection for the other person grow. When we are supported at crucial moments, rather than undermined, we are more receptive to other levels of honesty at other times. In this way, support, like talking, becomes a fundamental cornerstone in any good ongoing relationship between husband and wife.

3

Arguments: Methods in Madness

Stand, Simmer, or Boil?

My mother tells a story, which occurred in the fruit-growing country of the midwestern United States. It's about a young farmer's wife who learned to cope with her husband's temper in a unique way, visible to the entire local community. The husband, Herman, owned a fruit orchard and had a passion for apple pie. After five years of marriage, his wife finally realized that the shortest path to the end of any argument went via Herman's stomach. Consequently, whenever he came home fuming—she lit the oven and started a pie crust. Her solution prompted a brother-in-law neighbor to observe: "You can always tell when Herman has blown his stack, because you'll see smoke coming out of his chimney."

There are infinite ways of blowing one's stack and dealing with the heat generated from arguments: Some couples prefer retreating in the face of charged situations to allow for a cooling-off period. Others find themselves exploding at the drop of any sensitive idea—like politics or privacy or paying the bills.

Regardless of style, however, when the tumult or silence begins, something happens to all of us in the midst of battle. Hormones pump and blood pressure rises. There is a blending of fury with hurt and indignation. There is a feeling of every emotion but indifference. There is a brilliant display of spoken or unspoken fireworks. And that familiar voice of a fourteen-year-old adolescent, buried within most of us, cries out in spite of our best intentions.

Whether couples prefer to attack or withdraw in a fight, arguments tend to be painful and intense experiences. But a good fight, like good sex, includes a rhythm of tension, crescendo, climax, release, and exhaustion. *To stand, simmer, or boil is only part of the tension.* I think that relief in most arguments depends upon further acts, such as discussing, rediscussing, holding, crying, and very often, a special kind of lovemaking, that lead to feelings of closeness between two people.

Thus, how we handle our anger at the peak of an argument seems a highly individual matter and is touched upon only briefly in one section ("Concern—Kill 'em in Private"). The major focus of this chapter is on (1) ways to prevent arguments over false issues, (2) ways to resolve hostilities during a fight as well as after it, and (3) an overview of the positive role of arguments in intimacy.

In the Midst of Battle: Concern—Kill 'em in Private

We've all had the experience of saying something hurtful and lasting in the heat of an argument. Not only does it hurt to be hit below the belt, but such injuries are rarely helpful to inflict upon the person closest to us. I think that favorite four- or twelve-letter words aimed at each other are best expressed as thoughts, daydreams, fantasies, curses, silent outbursts, and unspoken epithets. (As was mentioned in "Which Honesty Is the Best Policy?" page 28.)

Here, it might be useful if we separate anger into two parts: thoughts and words. Our thoughts are frequently childish, hilarious, violent, and devastating. Still, our daydreams are the appropriate place to slay dragons and each other; our fantasies are a harmless way to vent uncensored infantile rage; and our silent cursing can bring indirect relief to us *without direct attacks on the personality of someone we love.*

Words are also a proper showcase in which to display anger. However, when fighting, negative *issues* are better to discuss than negative personalities. Global complaints are best translated into *specific comments.* The following examples illustrate the difference between what we might think and what we might say:

Thinking: "What a bitch!"
Saying: "What in the hell was going on with you at the party tonight?"

Thinking: "That's a part of you I've always hated."
Saying: "You spend every weekend finding nit-picky stuff I've done wrong around the house. Your drip-drip-drip complaints are worse than the Chinese water torture."

Thinking: "You're always so goddamned selfish."
Saying: "For Chrissake—you've only thought about yourself these past five days."

Thinking: "Why did we ever get married?"
Saying: "When I look at these bills, I could kill you."

Thinking: "I don't love you anymore."
Saying: "We're a million miles apart. We'd better talk before it's too late."

The difference in these examples between global attacks on personalities and specific attacks on issues may seem like a fine line. But, when a person emerges from an argument with the message: "I'm a bitch" or "bastard" or "selfish" or "unloved" his or her character is undermined and the ensuing hurt is a lasting one. The line between private thoughts and public pronouncements is measured, I believe, by a couple's concern for one another's feelings. This concern, not unlike the safety catch on a gun, acts to prevent the accidental discharge of loaded ammunition. With such protection, anger becomes a safer emotion. To know our secret weapons won't go off in public makes it easier to handle them in private.

And, in all honesty, our loaded feelings should not only be handled, but enjoyed: It should be fun to elaborate upon those "If only I'd said . . ." fantasies; those "bastards" and "sons-of-bitches" that pop up in the best of marriages; those images of throwing wine in our loved one's face or swinging from the chandelier shouting obscenities at everyone; those flashes of wanting to run from one's marriage, house, children, from, as Alexis Zorba says, "the full catastrophe."

Fatigue: The Universal Allergy

One of the most universal components of our arguments is fatigue.

Couples who are in the habit of working twelve-hour days, raising families or raising incomes, must pay the price of chronic exhaustion. For many people, their daily toll is so expensive that nothing is left over for nightly expenditures: No time is left to make conversation; no energy is available to make love. Consequently, fatigue raises hell in a vast majority of intimate relationships.

Most of us break out in rashes of irritability when we are tired, let alone exhausted. A husband may be irritated because he arrives home to a chilled wife and no martini; a tired wife may be irritated because her tardy husband begins every sentence with: "I, I, me, me, or my, my."

In many families, when evening arrives an exhausted pair needs to let-down at the same time. During the day, pressures have built and a couple's nightly needs often come into direct conflict: One person's desire to talk, another's desire for privacy. One's need to unwind, the other's inability to listen. One's wish to share his day, the other's wish to forget it. And so it goes. With the result: Irritants ooze, anger leaks, feelings overflow, and we suddenly find ourselves believing that our partner is selfish, self-centered, and slowly trying to kill us.

Although we cannot eliminate fatigue or end arguments, we can interrupt their cause-and-effect relationship. In recognizing our universal allergy to this human condition, I believe that we can reduce our hypersensitive reactions to one another by taking two positive steps:

Identifying the patterns: Many couples feel confused when their arguments seem unpredictable in their intensity and timing. Yet, certain predictable times—before menstrual periods, during in-law visits, after monthly bills, the final two hours of children, or the first two days of vacation—spell trouble for most families.

Couples who look for patterns to their fights may discover that some causes are obvious and that certain effects are predictable. Such predictability, in turn, allows the couple a degree of control over the situation; and it opens for them new ways of preventing recurrent arguments.

Let's take the obvious, if frequently overlooked, example of couples' repeatedly fighting on weekends. Two people who find themselves engaged in repetitious weekly battles might ask the simple question: "What is today?" Should the answer be, more-often-than-not, Friday night (or Sunday morning) couples have taken an important first step in resolving the problem.

Interrupting the fatigue/fight cycle: Those who recognize a familiar pattern in the above example might consider labeling it "The Friday Night (Sunday Morning) Syndrome" and also consider any of the following interventions to prevent it:

"If we talk now, it will end in disaster. Can't we be quiet for an hour?"

"You want to fight; I don't. Let's discuss it tomorrow."
"Look, it's Friday evening. Let's not argue tonight."
"What about a movie?"
"Why don't you take a bath before dinner?"
"Why don't we take a hot bath (together) after dinner?"
"Let's eat out. Have friends over. Go to bed early."

In this simplified example, what husband and wife learn in the process of aborting a Friday night fight is to avoid confrontations triggered by fatigue. This knowledge will save more than just wear and tear on Friday evenings or Sunday mornings. Practiced regularly, it can spare couples those hours upon hours of painful and pointless arguments, which are one predictable result of individual or mutual exhaustion, regardless of its source.

Bringing Trouble Home

Unfortunately, for most of us, our work is not the appropriate place to display true feelings which are negative or critical. The rewards for such honesty are few. Consequently, our daily frustrations are often swallowed which can lead to misdirected anger at home. For example:

Mr. Q, an intelligent and competitive scholar, advanced in fifteen years from his graduate studies to a university presidency. In achieving this meteoric success, Mr. Q always kept calm in the kill-or-be-killed atmosphere on campus. In fact, his greatest talent was to speak quietly in crises, handling faculty and students with respect and authority. Because of his position, as well as his ambition, Mr. Q never showed the unmitigated rage he often felt. Instead, his temper was saved for home.

To relieve his tension, Mr. Q would dilute his nightly anger with a bottle of Scotch and then direct his pent-up fury toward his wife. Many times, he would polish off both of them in the same evening.

Threatened by divorce, however, Mr. Q began to change. The

nature of one minor shift was the channeling of his overflowing
feelings away from his wife and onto the playing fields. He
found partners in handball, tennis, basketball, and bridge; and,
being a tough loser, Mr. Q soon became a killer on the courts as
well as at the card tables.

Finally, with his "outside" anger intruding less, Mr. Q's marital troubles—overshadowed by work for many years—were more
open to solution. Admittedly, this episode was only a small part
of a complicated history. Yet, it clearly demonstrates a human
tendency in married life: To translate pressures at work into
punishment (for our partner) at home.

From anger to action

There are several ways for us to protect our spouse from dis-
placed aggression and accusation. When we make time in the
evening to jog, putter, garden, cook, paint, write (angry letters
to the editor), hit golf balls, or play music, our eight-to-five frustrations tend to be absorbed and detoxified in such activities.
Troubles at work, or with children, are still discussed at night;
but daily tiffs and battles, compromises or failures are simply
not blamed on each other.

Such actions do not mean that all negative feelings should be
redirected into outside activities. Obviously, normal frustrations
unrelated to the relationship will intrude in spite of our best intentions to protect the person we love. But, whereas it may feel
good to yell at our wife, explode at our husband, snap at the
dog, it's clearly unhelpful to make a habit of using each other
as scapegoats for problems outside the home.

Making Decisions

What about resolving difficulties within the household?

Let us begin at a relatively simple level: There are chores and
routines in the daily operation of any home: the chores of

emptying garbage or feeding the cat, routines of locking up at night or opening a bedroom window. These are neutral functions over which daily skirmishes are often fought. How wide should the window be opened at bedtime? Who carries out the trash or feeds a pet? Who checks doors and opens windows? Should two lovers find themselves repeatedly bickering over these or similar mundane duties, they might find it helpful to discuss the problem, especially when not angry over it, and make a decision about future responsibility.

Who is responsible?

When couples continually make "much to do about nothing," it may be relatively easy to settle the conflict by asking and answering: "Who does what?"

Ed and Alice, married three and one-half years without children, bought a little dachshund. Not untypically, during their first month with the new pet, they would argue at bedtime:

Ed: Did you feed the puppy?

Alice: Me? I thought you did it.

Ed: I'm tired—I forgot.

Alice: I'm exhausted, too.

Ed: Should I go?

Alice: (*martyred*) No, I will. (*But first tell me that it's your fault!*)

For two weeks this dialogue became a nightly ritual and source of irritation to husband and wife. Ed would say after dinner: "Is the dog fed?" To which Alice always replied, "Not yet. Don't bug me. I'm busy—you're not."

The situation improved when Alice decided to take charge of everyone's supper . . . including the dachshund. After her interrogation started the next evening, Alice told Ed: "Stop asking.

It's my responsibility. I'll do it." Ed didn't raise the question again and the mini-crisis with their first newborn came to an end.

Here, the reader might properly object to the over-simplification of such an example. He may think Alice is saying "All right, I'll feed the dog" simply to keep the peace. She doesn't honestly believe feeding the pet is her job and is really simmering:

"Hell, I'll do it. But why am I always the one to do everything?"
"Just because I'm the woman . . ."
"I don't mind feeding Ed, but he's the one who likes dogs."
"Who needs a pet when there's so much else to be done?"

Alice may remain calm on the surface. But, one day—weeks or months later—she might blow-up out of all proportion when Ed asks: "Hey, love, did you pick up my laundry today?" All because she's made that compromise with the damn dog. Having won that minor skirmish, Ed now expects his wife to accept an endless series of minor responsibilities (such as dropping his shirts, picking them up, picking up mail, and so forth).

Alice's feelings of martyrdom ("I don't like it, but I'll do it . . .") are certainly common in the best of marriages from time to time. The reality is that daily living does involve a continuing routine of trivial chores, which someone must do! However, compromises over those chores ("Okay, I'll feed the puppy . . . you clean up his poops.") become easier, I believe, in an atmosphere of shared responsibility and mutual cooperation. It doesn't get any simpler, for example, if the husband thinks: "I'm responsible for making the money, you be responsible for everything else."

On the other hand: Even with good feelings about the give-and-take at home, I'm not sure we ever get to "like" the mundane tasks. (Be it cleaning out toilet bowls or cleaning up dog poops.) But, at least we don't have to hate it. Or more accurately, with mutual cooperation, we don't have to translate resentments about the chores into resentments about our mate. My point is not that shared responsibility means an exact 50/50 split, an unyielding quid pro quo, a written contract. But rather, I'm implying a *spirit of helpfulness* between two people who basically desire to please the person they love. (Regarding the larger compromises between lovers, see "Faking It," page 85 and "Doing What Comes (Un)Naturally," page 110.)

Who is talented?

In many cases, "Who is responsible?" is decided by asking: "Who can do (rather than should do) the best job? To put it another way: Responsibility can be determined by a person's skill instead of his sex. Consequently, in repetitive fights, it helps to decide: Who is more talented in this particular situation? For whom is the problem easier?

When a husband, who worked as an editor, asked his wife "for the 4,276th time" if she had written some thank you notes, the wife decided to end his nagging and her own excuses. She was tired of a running battle over saying "thank you." Asking her husband to shift gears and reverse roles, the wife took a common-sense approach: "It's easy for you to write and it's hard for me. Lord knows—I've tried. From this note on, why don't you assume my role as family correspondent?" While contrary to most standards of etiquette, this couple's small shift of responsibilities proved helpful to them. It clarified an ongoing problem, offered a solution, and ended a minor—but chronic—argument.

My feeling is that conflicts over major responsibilities—such as the handling of money—can initially be attacked in the same way. In deciding who is most talented, couples need to evaluate their own strengths and weaknesses based upon a realistic appraisal of past experience. Two people are more effective (in writing thank-you notes or balancing budgets) if they can admit individual skills in the situation without anger or defensiveness.

On financial matters, for example: If a husband or wife can trim expenses, set limits on expenditures, and save money better than does his partner—why shouldn't the couple invest in the most talented person the responsibility for finances? Should one person be less adept at handling money, so what? His traits of spending or generosity, or his inability to say "no," can be discussed without rancor. Hopefully, the result will be one person's expertise with money helping to lower a couple's monthly bills, as well as their shouting over them.

My point is not that such a decision will end financial difficulties in the household. Not at all. But, it may help to decrease arguments over a variety of false issues in the battles over checkbooks, credit cards, and charge accounts.

A brief word about money—or the lack of it. Money remains in the top one or two most common reasons given for divorce. Few aspects of a relationship are more charged or complicated. Dollars and cents represent different values to different people: Power and control, status and sexuality, freedom and security, happiness and misery. Money can be a symbol for all feelings. However, it can also be a reality for couples in love, since the pursuit of money is often costly to most styles of intimacy. As such, the problems of "Values: Time As Well As Money" will be the subject of Chapter 6.

Taking a Stand

What happens if fights last beyond the ten- or fifteen-round limit, being refought over and over without any final decision?

Couples who experience continual assaults on their values or personality may counterattack with self-defeating patterns of self-defense. Venting their frustration after two days or twenty years of the same problem, they explode with threats, such as: "If you don't . . . I'm leaving." Or, turning a deaf ear on long-playing arguments, they become indifferent to resolving the underlying issue. Or worse, they become indifferent to their husband or wife.

The danger lies not in couples' thinking "Stop! No more!" but in the way they choose to express it. By threats or indifference, people tend to direct anger at each other, instead of the stimulus that ignited their angry response in the first place. Energy is so consumed in return bouts of the same old fight that both are left drained and defeated. In such battles, there are no winners.

What is the difference between these tactics and taking a stand in perpetual arguments? Hopefully, taking stands—"drawing the line," "putting one's foot down,"—focuses on problems, not personalities. As the strong, often childish expression of likes and dislikes, it is part of that valuable feedback so necessary to two people living together. Saying "Never again . . . " or "From now on . . . " may be empty phrases. Or, they may teach a couple to know what a loved-one values and to appreciate the limits of his willingness to compromise.

Some readers may not see the difference between a "stand" and an "ultimatum" or "threat." Yet, the concept need not be so negative. At its best, I think, the notion of taking a stand is more analogous to setting limits in a relationship. As such, it is no more a threat than when a mother says to her child, "You can yell at the baby, but don't poke him in the eye with your finger." Whereas it can be helpful in innumerable parent-child situations to set limits (are they not one expression of concern and caring?); so, too, it can be helpful as adults to tell the person we love about our own limits. For example:

From time to time, the following dialogue may occur in families during a crisis. Be it over a minor or major stumbling block.

Chronic Argument Number 1:

Partner "A": (*dining-out with friends*) Oh stupid! You've asked the difference between red and white wine at the last three restaurants.

Partner "B": *(afterwards)* You can criticize me in private. But, don't you ever, EVER! criticize me again in public.

Chronic Argument Number 2:

Partner "A": You remember so and so? Well, I'm having dinner with him (her) this Thursday night.

Partner "B": I thought we'd decided that Christmas cards are okay. But that neither of us would see past lovers on any basis, even as so-called friends. I want you to cancel dinner.

Chronic Argument Number 3:

Partner "A": We're having guests on Friday and Saturday nights. On Sunday, we're invited for dinner. Sorry, darling, but I couldn't avoid it.

Partner "B": One invitation per weekend is reasonable. But three are ridiculous. No more accepting invitations until we discuss them.

Chronic Argument Number 4:

Partner "A": You drive me nuts by not being on time.

Partner "B": Look! For three years we've argued about time. I've done my best to please you, but there's a limit. I'm now so worried about being late that I'm always a half hour early. It's time for you to change.

One partner's ability to "stand up" for himself may lead to basic shifts by a loved-one, *if* he values and honors the convictions behind his partner's stand. Thus, *if respected,* a person's strong feelings not only help to end arguments but also to preserve the individual's own convictions and self-esteem. In taking a stand, one's personal integrity is fortified rather than violated.

And in maintaining their individual integrity, a husband and wife move closer to preserving the integrity of their relationship.

Ending the Silent Treatment

Not infrequently, two people reach a stalemate at the beginning, middle, or end of an argument and they withdraw into the initial comfort of silence. Comfort, however, soon turns to discomfort, and most of us find it remarkably hard to end our subsequent cold wars. For instance, if the silent treatment lasts for hours (or days), we share a mutual wish for the other person to apologize. We make secret vows, admittedly foolish, not to speak until spoken to. It is not uncommon for us to think in private:

Wife: There's no point in talking until he apologizes.

Husband: Why can't she speak first?

Wife: Just admit you were wrong.

Husband: I could say "I'm sorry" . . . but I won't.

Wife: So, say "Boo" . . . say anything.

Husband: I refuse to be the one who gives in.

Wife: This is ridiculous.

Husband: This is crazy.

How to resolve the impasse?

When our righteous indignation leads to more childishness and greater tension, there are at least two helpful steps we can take to begin talking:

Eliminate the power struggle: Couples must learn that the question: "To speak or not to speak?" need not be the same as "To lose or not to lose?" There is a common tendency to feel: "If I speak first, he wins." With the result, sparring partners conclude that silences must always end with winners and losers; either a man's victory and woman's defeat; or her innocence and his guilt. This need "to win" undermines most peace efforts and continues the power struggle. The following ice-breaking lines tend to be unhelpful in reconciling differences:

"You've ruined my day, but . . . "
"You're out of your mind . . . "
"Have you looked in the mirror lately?"
"Did you listen to your voice? Boy, talk about being bitchy!"
"Isn't it time that you had a little talk with yourself?"

Such remarks tend to infuriate the opposition. Again, the fight becomes a question of attack and defense in pursuit of ultimate victory. And in the process, wounds are reopened instead of healed.

To start talking, one person must accept responsibility for ending the power struggle. He must avoid battles of will. He must not really care who saves face or who loses it. Consequently, he must initiate any of the following remarks to begin the painful task of breaking a silence.

"I'm sorry."
"I apologize."
"I didn't mean to get so mad."
"Okay, I'm stupid and an idiot, but don't be mad at me tonight."
"Let's talk."

Or, if these comments are too risky, a person can avoid the problem of "right" and "wrong" with a neutral statement, such as: "Frankly, if this is the worst of our problems—we're in good shape."

Many times it is easier to forget the words which may be awkward or uncomfortable in the situation, and reach our partner with a thoughtful gesture. Especially when two people reach the point where each is just looking for an excuse to end the whole childish episode, a passing squeeze, an unexpected touch, a certain smile all help to signal a truce and restore tranquility. Breaking the ice with these verbal or nonverbal actions tends to reduce mounting tension and relieve everyone.

The elimination of power struggles, an admittedly difficult process, usually reopens the broken lines of communication. Successful or not, however, it is helpful to proceed with a second step.

Set limits and make a house rule: Few couples find it pleasant to remain distant for endless hours or days. Few people enjoy the sinking feeling: "The longer this silence goes on, the worse it gets." Indeed, most husbands and wives who must keep their head above troubled waters relax only when they can measure the distance to safety. My belief is that ends to fights provide the same relief as do edges to swimming pools. They offer the individual security and protection. Consequently, it makes sense that two people set limits on their arguments.

When a pair repeatedly think:

"Here we go again. I'm sleeping on the couch."
or
"I can't stand it. Maybe I'll leave home for a few days."
or
"There goes another night shot to hell."

The following house rule can be established: *We never go to sleep angry.*

This rule allows couples to fight with a time limit on their arguments. A person who thinks, "Will this silence never end?" need not face days or weeks of unlimited debate. Indeed, he can feel secure in knowing: Hostilities are to be confined to waking hours. Arguments must be resolved before sleep.

The reality, of course, is that we do climb into bed angry at each other. So, for the house rule to work, further steps are necessary: On silent nights, one person must break the impasse by saying, "Are we going to fall asleep this way?" or, by repeating the rule, "I thought we weren't going to go to bed mad." Then starts, even at this late hour, the laborious process of airing woes . . . of exchanging grievances . . . of talking. It sounds exhausting. It is exhausting. Yet, I know of no substitute for this kind of effort, to make peace before bedtime.

Clearly, this house rule is a skill requiring years of trial and error and living together. It cannot become a reality without practice. Even with practice, however, sometimes it is just too hard. Nonetheless, I believe it is worth striving for such a goal . . . worth instigating a simple house rule, which can ring the final bell at night—a time to lower defenses and come out talking.

A Time for Distance,
a Time for Closeness

A realistic part of living together consists of experiencing powerful and opposite feelings. Feelings of tenderness, as well as hurt; of sharing, as well as selfishness; of understanding, as well as misunderstanding; of closeness, as well as distance. In the private world between husband and wife there comes a time for every emotion under the sun. Or, as it was originally described in Ecclesiastes:

> A time for birth, a time for death,
> a time to plant, and a time to uproot,
> a time to kill, a time to heal,
> a time to break down, and a time to build,
> a time to cry, a time to laugh,
> a time to mourn, a time to dance,
> a time to scatter, and a time to gather,
> a time to embrace, a time to refrain,
> a time to seek, a time to lose,
> a time to keep, a time to cast away,
> a time to tear, a time to sew,
> a time for silence, and a time for speech,
> a time for love, a time for hate,
> a time for war, a time for peace.

What is the role of anger in this ebb and flow of life? How does it relate to the swinging of the pendulum between such opposite poles?

Does anger not increase when the pendulum has swung too far in one direction? When two people have drifted apart, becoming distant over time? Time measured by isolation, not intimacy; by boredom, not stimulation; by fatigue, not fulfillment; by speaking, not listening; by things, not each other? And if true, does rising anger not reflect, at one level, growing coolness and distance in a couple's relationship?

Anger as a signal: Paradoxically, hate or hurt can signal a time to restore closeness. When arguments heat up in frequency or intensity, they can signal a need to make time for each other. Time to be alone; time to talk without other people. Time to say "no" (to cancel engagements and to set limits on acquaintances, visitors, house guests, even friends). Time to get away from children. Time to spend a weekend in the mountains or by the sea. Time to touch; to share secrets; to reminisce; to smile; to fill up; to make love. Time to be nourished.

One key to translating feelings of anger into feelings of intimacy is perspective; viewing arguments not only as normal, frustrating, infuriating, and often humiliating experiences; *but also,* recognizing anger as a helpful signal.

This view adds a positive dimension to negative feelings. If we use this framework, anger can serve as a thermostat of closeness and distance in maintaining intimacy. And, viewed in this perspective, arguments can help to enrich our lives while preserving the rhythm and balance in our relationship.

Sexual Fantasies: For Lovers Only

It is not inconsistent for couples who are happily married to enjoy a wild fantasy life. Like most people they will go to a party, pick up the sexual vibrations of a friend or stranger . . . and imagine the best. Wives respond in erotic ways to other men and husbands react in sensual ways to other women. My feeling is that such hidden thoughts can act to enrich a marriage.

Whereas sexual fantasies may be a pleasure, they can also arouse mixed emotions. They can bubble up at unexpected times to add confusion, pain, guilt, or spice to the Walter Mitty in everyone. When making love, for example, most young lovers share the common fantasy of calling their sexual partner by the wrong name in the middle of intercourse. At an early point in one's sex life, most people say to themselves:

"God, what if I made a mistake . . . ?"
"If someone tapped me on the shoulder and asked who I was loving,
   I could just as easily say 'Herb' as 'David.'"
"So I won't use names . . . "

Obviously, such thoughts are best experienced in private. These ideas are embarrassing to admit, unhelpful to announce, and not particularly appropriate to discuss with the person we love.

Chapter 4's purpose is to describe various ways that our imagination can become (or continue as) a silent partner and secret ally in our fight against individual and sexual boredom. Let us begin with some common examples of fantasies.

Fantasies of Everyday Life

Married or not, a man's daydreams are stimulated when an attractive woman enters his life. Even for a moment. Of course, some men are reluctant to admit these fantasies (even to themselves). Their thoughts often stir erotic feelings that result in denial.

For example, don't we all enjoy the bra-less hitchhiker extending her thumb and other protrusions, but don't we also pretend that she isn't the main reason for driving home the longer way? Don't we stare in disbelief at this year's Lolitas exhibiting themselves at the high school crosswalk, but don't we hide our two roving eyes behind one very straight face? On trips alone, don't we imagine ten thoughts for every word spoken to that understanding stewardess or seatmate, cocktail waitress or chambermaid? And don't we doctors think beyond the sensuous patient's trouble as she reveals its location? Doesn't her plumber? Don't most men? But instead, don't we talk to her seriously about pain or plumbing or the chance of rain?

For men *or women*, daily fantasies are triggered by people, events, and past experiences. They are a return to adolescent turmoil without the same pain, but with similar fears: "If he talks to me, what do I say?" They are ignited by explosive and unpredictable thoughts, such as: "If I were dying . . . ?" or "If he died, who would I . . . ?" Fantasies are a surge of vague feelings, a silent language, for which there is no adequate translation: a mixture of chemistry and hormones, of logic and madness.

Daily fantasies are triggered in seconds. And they usually last only seconds. These fleeting moments become special moments when our glance is exchanged; when the moment is shared;

when the feeling is mutual. In the midst of a boring day, such fantasies are bursts of welcomed excitement; of coming alive and feeling alive for the first time in hours (or months). They are reminders in everyday life of the joys of feeling aroused, of feeling inspired, of feeling sexual.

Fantasies of Expectation

Before marriage, young couples are stimulated by the rituals of preparing for a "date" on Saturday night. Hot tubs and bathroom mirrors provide the setting for their great expectations. Plans for the seduction often begin early in the evening: The woman may start to feel excited as she washes her hair, shaves her legs, and picks out a matching set of black underwear.

A man, in his naïve ways, accepts the responsibility for ending up in bed. His shower and shave is a time to plot strategy: When drinks? Where dinner? And how to move from frying pan to fireside? He dreams of being smooth in word, skillful in deed, and slowly running his fingers over a black slip, black bra, and black pants. (When seduced, however, he fails to appreciate the coincidence or counterplot!) Such fantasies are erotic for a man and woman regardless of the evening's outcome. The fact is that these sexual expectations start an evening with hope and drama, which is one of the great pleasures of an unmarried person's going out on Saturday or any other night.

Let us now turn to long-term relationships and ask: In marriage, how can such adulteries of our mind prove helpful to the actions in our bed?

Fantasies and Boredom:
Old Friends and New Possibilities

After several years or several children, married couples find life—including Saturday nights—to be predictable instead of unpredictable. In fact, the predictability of everyday living is a major cause of sexual boredom. (As is aging, illness, fatigue, anger, preoccupations, or rigid lovemaking. See also Chapter 5 which is devoted to the problem of sexual boredom.) During periods of boring sex, many people find themselves imagining the "good old days" or dreaming about a new life. For instance:

A husband in a four-year marriage was unhappy at bedtime. The source of his frustration was obvious and lay between him and his wife—she was nine months pregnant.

In the first trimester of pregnancy and again now, the would-be mother became nauseated at the thought of fish, red wine, or sex. The husband loved his wife, but hated the pregnancy. Intercourse was not only boring, it was almost nonexistent. During his nights of celibate sleep, the husband would dream at length. And his prior sexual history was a great comfort. He would review old girl friends and past seasons almost compulsively every night. Like a football coach, he spent the dreaming hours in recalling the details of each victory, repeating the key plays over and over in his imagination.

Is this phenomenon peculiar to the male? No, I don't think so. In nightdreams as well as daydreams, women also enjoy their sexual fantasies. One familiar example: Ten minutes after Mr. L left home in the morning, Mrs. L, a thirty-one-year-old mother and housewife, would get depressed. She would face the breakfast dishes and feel overwhelmed by the monotony of her next nine hours.

One day, while stopping at the neighborhood laundromat, Mrs. L saw a very tall and very handsome red-haired young man. Quite suddenly, she was surprised and overpowered by the flood of her sexual feelings for the man. She considered smiling at him, speaking to him, or continuing to fold clothes. And she debated the question: "What if he actually turned to say, 'Come with me.' "

The fantasy of escaping to a new life shook Mrs. L from a

state of emptiness to a feeling of excitement. At first, the impulses were frightening to her—but she was soon enjoying them. With cheeks flushed and heart pounding, she imagined the drama of telling her husband, "Oh, I am sorry, darling . . . but I'm in love with another man. I'll be leaving you tonight . . . with a full drawer of clean socks. Good-bye, Love, good-bye."

Departing the laundromat, Mrs. L blushed at feeling so good. Her boredom had quickly vanished and she found herself plotting the rest of the day. With the result that when Mr. L came home tired that night, a special dinner was awaiting him. And later, he discovered a passionate stranger in bed.

Although this incident is clearly over-simplified, what was so helpful about the laundromat fantasy?

When a woman is cast in the role of housewife, she cannot escape from boredom. She cannot feel attractive or erotic in the middle of morning dishes or dirty socks. And yet, in fact or fantasy, she needs to experience herself not only as a stable wife to one man, but as a sexual woman to many men. In fantasy, her needs can be silently met without causing damage to her husband and without having to discuss the source of her inspiration. In short, she grows more confident with all the applause she can get—real or imagined. And, it is a simple truth that when a woman no longer feels dead *on* her feet, she is less likely to feel dead *off* of them.

At this point, we might ask: How do women, or men, learn to expand their sexual fantasies? Why are they so restricted in some marriages? What helps us to daydream—in bed as well as out of it?

Limiting Fantasies I:
Out of Bed

The problem of how to expand fantasies can be solved, in part, by asking the opposite question: How are fantasies restricted? To answer the question, let us begin with a brief look at the experience of watching pornographic films and burlesque shows.

Skin flicks and strippers

Although pornographic movies are an obviously complicated subject, they provide, in one sense, a good example of fantasy production in reverse. Most viewers enter such films with high hopes and erotic expectations. Once seated, they wait impatiently for "the good parts." Tension mounts, pressure builds, and suddenly there explodes on the screen a plethora of forbidden parts and positions; a smorgasbord for every taste: solo performances, duets, quartets, sextets, and more.

Yet, in spite of these infinite possibilities, many viewers find one common denominator in skin flicks (beyond their shock value). Films tend to channel even the most overflowing imagination into narrow outlets. Especially with today's telescopic lenses, a person's attention is focused upon the minutest details of breasts and nipples, vaginas and vulvas. Human anatomy and intercourse is scrutinized at such close range that it destroys beyond recognition the individual's view of lovemaking. He is simply overwhelmed by penises and pubic hair and asses everywhere.

In blue movies, the advertisements are right: "Nothing is left to your imagination."

Although old burlesque shows didn't go "all the way," they provoked similar reactions: Curtains opened with fanfares, whistles, and catcalls. The "tease" in striptease meant that "anything goes." And, in the beginning, it did. The stripper's fully clad body left *everything* to one's imagination.

But the show had to go on. So, as the old (or young) pro gradually removed her fans, bubbles, or clothes—audiences were slowly robbed of their illusions. The more anatomy she revealed, the fewer of their daydreams remained. And by the time her G-string hit the dust, so had the audience's fantasies. In the end, illusionless men found little to applaud at the final curtain.

I do not mean that erotic "art forms" never whet one's appetite. For many people, fantasies are stimulated by the process of watching burlesque queens and hard-core movie heroes. For most of us, there is excitement in viewing naked performers and performances, especially when they engage in previously forbidden acts. However, as the forbidden becomes familiar, excitement turns to emptiness. With repeated exposure, most viewers would agree that there is little fun in watching the fourth stripper (or fourth orgy). By then, erotic shows have become monotonous rituals. And an expensive night has turned into a boring one.*

Limiting Fantasies II:
In Bed

If graphic details on stage or screen limit a person's fantasies (at the moment), so do his specific preoccupations in bed. The more he is preoccupied with realities—Did I set the alarm? Lock the car? Take my pill? Will the neighbors hear us? Will the children?—the less likely he is to fantasize.

Some obvious distractions during sex are the result of physical illness. Common colds are distracting because they interfere with breathing, swallowing, and kissing. Broken limbs are distracting because they add to intercourse the nuisance of positioning a cast. Bad backs are distracting because they hurt with the slight-

* Supporting this view is the recent experience in Denmark. The overwhelming majority of Danish people, after nearly four years of giving free reign to pornography, are now ignoring it. From the peak of 72 million dollars in 1969 to the 28 million dollars in 1971, their "porno industry" is now selling ninety per cent of its products to tourists from the more restrictive countries or to foreign mail buyers. "The Danes have worked through several phases, each culminating in a yawn of uninterest." Initially, there is great excitement—followed by a let down. For example, Copenhagen's first "Sex Fair," attracted charter planeloads from as far away as Cairo and New York. The second one, in 1971, was a money-losing failure. ("Living with Pornography: The Danish Experience," by Roy Perrott, London Observer, reprinted in the San Francisco Chronicle, September 19, 1971.)

est movement. Pregnancies are distracting because they come between two people in more ways than one.

Fortunately, these physical preoccupations tend to be time-limited. Although the disabilities of one's body may cause temporary distractions at bedtime—colds do resolve, bones mend, backs heal, pregnancies end. And in throwing away the crutches, Kleenex, or maternity clothes, a person is again able to experience, more freely, internal sensations and feelings other than his own pain or discomfort.

Once healthy, of course, individuals may be distracted by a wide range of surprising and unpredictable thoughts. This is classically the case when two people go to bed with each other for the first time. As relative strangers, they often conceal hidden reservations about the other person or about their own performance. The abbreviated scene below is not uncommon.

A young nurse felt lonely at the umpteenth party she'd attended since her recent divorce from an eight-year marriage. On this particular night, however, she met a sympathetic teacher and left with him to talk at his apartment. There, one drink led to another and soon the couple began to neck, pet, and undress.

Meanwhile, both were preoccupied.

The man thought: "A nurse—she must be on the pill. How do I ask? What do I say? Maybe she'll tell me first. Oh, the hell with it. Actually, she doesn't look as good without her clothes. Still, I shouldn't have drunk so much tonight. The question is: Can I last? And good grief, how do I get out of this when it's over?"

The nurse thought: "This isn't what I had in mind at all. What am I doing here?"

In spite of the fact that the nurse and her friend may be acting on previous fantasies ("Some enchanted evening . . . you may

see a stranger . . . across a crowded room . . . "), present fantasies will have trouble breaking past their current barrier of silent
preoccupations and fears.

The experience of lovemaking is diluted for any couple—be it
for the first or four hundredth time—when their attention is
directed elsewhere. Sex is less erotic when a man's time is spent
in thinking about obtaining and maintaining his erection or not
getting his partner pregnant. Intercourse is less fun when the
woman's energy is spent in worrying about her image, orgasm,
odor, lubrication, or menstruation. The same is true when either
person is preoccupied about fatigue, money, neighbors, noise,
children, diet, weight, or whatever. With such expenditures of
time and energy, couples cannot afford the luxury of a fantasy
life.

Consciously or unconsciously, when a person is preoccupied
during sex, he cannot relax and "let it be." With distractions
on his mind, he is less likely to let go in the midst of intercourse.
He cannot dissolve his body image; and he cannot lose himself
in another person, another experience, another world.

In Someone Else's Bed I:
Report of a Case

Many extramarital affaires, if the facts were known, could easily
be described as "stranger than truth." The following case occurred in a large New England city and is one unadulterated
example.

For six months, Mrs. O kept secret "the other man" in her
life. During that half year, Mrs. O would leave her husband to
meet her lover at an odd time: between one o'clock and five
o'clock in the morning. Such hours were chosen not because her
husband worked a graveyard shift, but because he was an incredibly heavy sleeper. After his fourteen-hour day, Mr. O barely

had the energy to finish dinner and make it into bed. Once there, he always slept like the dead.

On the other hand, Mrs. O's recently divorced friend practiced law Monday through Friday; he saw his three children every weekend; and besides, he wanted to see Mrs. O in the evenings. Consequently, she felt the night business, admittedly unorthodox, was the best alternative under the circumstances. (It also seemed the most foolproof way to sleep in two beds at once.)

One night, however, Mrs. O had an accident. She crept out of bed and left Mr. O as usual. But the drive across town to her lover's apartment proved almost fatal: She fell asleep, jumped the curb, hit a parking meter, smashed the car, broke her left wrist, and cracked some ribs. By 1:30 A.M., Mrs. O's boy friend responded to her call. By 2:00 A.M., they reached the hospital. By three, the fracture was set. By four, Mrs. O was scheduled for more X-rays of her rib cage. And by six, Mr. O would be awakening in an empty bed.

What to do?

Luckily, the physician, Dr. C, was a good friend of the attorney. So, between 4:00 and 4:30, the whole bizarre affair was explained to him. In the end, Dr. C reluctantly agreed to inform Mr. O of his wife's accident.

When the husband failed to answer his phone on the twentieth ring, it was obvious to all that Mrs. O was right in assuming her plan to be fail-safe. Yet, the question remained: How to tell Mr. O?

Dr. C drove the thirty minutes across town to the O's house, reaching their front gate at 5:15 in the morning. When two neighbor's dogs started barking, Dr. C was convinced that Mr. O would rise to the occasion. But he didn't. After a quarter hour of dogs' barking and doorbell's ringing, the expression "dead to the world" took on new significance. Eventually, at 5:30, Mr. O woke up. Still half-asleep, he just couldn't buy the story about his wife's accident. "Sorry, doctor, but you must be at the wrong house," he finally interrupted, "because *my* wife is still asleep in our bed. Now, if you'll excuse me, good night," and he closed the door. Returning to an empty bedroom, however, Mr. O finally woke up.

Later, at the hospital, secrets were revealed by Mrs. O's eventual confession.

In Someone Else's Bed II:
Limiting or Liberating?

Ideally, an extramarital affaire permits two lovers to enjoy very positive and gratifying rewards. To have an affaire is to feel aroused, excited, desirable, valued, and sexual. All good feelings. Theoretically, at least, such reactions could act as potent medicine for bored individuals as well as their boring marriages. In feeling alive, married lovers or mistresses could become alive with renewed vigor at home. In regaining self-esteem and self-confidence, they could breathe new life into themselves and their original mate.

Realistically, however, how many affaires have such therapeutic effect upon a marriage? And if not, why not?

By and large, affaires require that married participants not only cheat on their spouse, but lie to them as well. People must excuse late hours, make up half-truths about days off, and say "wrong number" to cancel the right phone call at an inappropriate time. Each day, if they are not being honest, they must cover all bases and keep straight what lie was told to which person. It's exhausting. As a result, the price of their storytelling is high. Cost to a relationship can be measured not only in hours spent with the third person, but also in effort used to play such games. Ultimately, individuals must borrow time and energy—both in limited supply—from their marriage to invest in their affaire.

And this drain on a couple's relationship only multiplies their existing problems at home.

In addition to demands on hours and energy, trouble may arise because of conflicting feelings—often the unwanted and unpleasant side effects of an affair. In such cases, liaisons may produce a nagging sense of discomfort in married men or women. Part of them views the extramarital business as distinctly out-of-character. They honestly entered marriage for better or worse, in sickness or health, and with monogamy in mind. At first, in someone else's bed, they have no intention of leaving their husband or wife. Later, in their own bed, they begin to feel like a stranger in no man's land. Lost between two worlds, they feel confused, lonely, anxious, embarrassed, guilty, hypocritical, and depressed. At this point, good feelings have become mixed with painful ones.*

In many cases, the double life eventually becomes too painful. Subsequently, people are forced into the position of fishing or cutting bait in their marriage. They have two basic choices: If they choose the marital relationship, they suffer for leaving the outside person who offered them an island of excitement midst their sea of boredom. On the other hand: If the extramarital relationship is chosen, they suffer for breaking up their family— with all of its implications. In either choice, the result includes unhappy feelings.

If the person elects to stop his affaire and stay in his marriage, both husband and wife may ask not only "Will it happen again?" but also "How to prevent repeated episodes?" And it is the answer to this last question that may affect the person's sexual fantasies.

For example, an individual may reasonably think: "I had sexual fantasies before the affaire. I acted upon these fantasies. In fact, I really enjoyed acting upon them. The affaire was good for me. But in the end, it caused too much pain for all three of

---

* I am aware that these generalizations have limited application and vary with the person's age, conscience, culture, and subculture.

us." Conclusion: "No more affaires." The simplified version of this inner logic might be diagrammed as follows:

romantic fantasies → extramarital affaire → conflicted feelings → "no more"

Mistresses or lovers might conclude that one logical place to break these events is at the starting point. They may think: "Daydreams are too scary. I might act on them. Better to put the lid on my adulterous fantasies. I'll just forget them. It's easier and safer that way." However, such reasoning puts the blame for painful feelings at the door of one's sexual fantasies. And herein lies the key to the problem.

Thoughts versus actions

To shut off daydreams in order to prevent extracurricular activity is based on a false assumption. It should be clear that private thoughts do not have to become public deeds; ideas need not be synonymous with acts; sensual fantasies are not equal to sexual affaires. To imply cause-and-effect relationships only leads to worse problems. Throwing out one's fantasies (like the perennial baby with the bath water) not only misses the point, but it is also foolish.

Consciously or unconsciously, when we bury our daydreams we set in motion a self-defeating cycle. We cut off a major flow of sexual inspiration and we ignore a rich source of variety in our lives. In blocking the pathways to our hidden fantasies, we deprive ourselves of spice and surprise in everyday living. As a result, we tend to feel increasingly bored at work and home. Boredom, in turn, leads to more pressure for an exciting interlude to break our spell of monotony. And, in the end, we are at the beginning of our problem. This chain of events might be diagrammed as follows:

↓ Fantasies → ↓ stimulation → ↑ boredom → ↑ need for sexual excitement → ↑ pressure to find action elsewhere.

In this case, however, the race toward an affaire does not begin with too many sexual fantasies. On the contrary. It starts with too few fantasies—or none at all.

Expanding Fantasies I: Permission

Once married, we often consider fantasies to be wrong. Most of us believe that a romance with one person should "cure" our adulterous ideas about many people. Frequently, we tend to view fantasies after marriage as signs of pathology rather than signs of health in our relationship. For instance, the following comments were mentioned in psychotherapy sessions.

A housewife married two years: "Occasionally I wake up at night dreaming about an old boyfriend. The specific details escape me, but the dream provokes very erotic feelings. When I realize my husband is asleep in bed next to me, I'm slightly ashamed and embarrassed to feel so good about my past sex life [which is usually much better in dreams than it ever was in reality]."

A graduate student married five years: "At first it bothered me to fantasize about other women during sex with my wife. But I soon discovered that it helped at times to pretend she was someone else. In fact, when I'm exhausted it may be the only way to get an erection and make lovemaking good for us both."

A divorce lawyer married ten years: "I know that my trouble with seductive clients means that I'm giving them an obvious come-on. As soon as I think the problem is licked, I find myself looking at some fantastic body and thinking how wild she could be in bed. I'm just too much! It really scares hell out of me."

A concert violinist married twenty-five years: "My husband and I have a good marriage. We enjoy a full life. But I see the kids today with all of their freedom—and I'm a little jealous. My God, whenever I notice an attractive man—which I've been doing now for thirty years—I still feel a little guilty about it. Can you imagine? Don't you agree this generation is luckier than ours? At least about sex?"

These comments from a variety of people are deceptively rare and illuminating. Rare, because few men and women discuss their sexual fantasies, even in a psychiatrist's office. Illuminating, because all of these individuals report some degree of guilt, embarrassment, shame, doubt, or fear in connection with this part of their inner world.

Let us ask here: "Why should married people view their sexual fantasies as improper, or worse immoral?"

Beyond the confusion of thoughts with deeds, I think one answer lies in our popular notions about marriage. As those romantic lyrics tell us: "I [should] only have eyes for you." Thus, we often grow up expecting that a love affair (especially marriage) will automatically shut off our fantasies about other people. Of course, fantasies do not end when marriage begins. Indeed, they are just starting. Consequently, it is natural to experience twinges of discomfort with our fantasies in the early stages of living together. Such feelings may not be so tangible as: "Something's wrong with the marriage." But rather, they produce vague and uneasy thoughts such as: "Something must be wrong with me," or "If everything were okay, why do I have such ideas?" Or, more simply: "This is outrageous."

We might ask: "Need something be wrong in the relationship? or in me?" "Why shouldn't I be free to fantasize? even to be outrageous?"

In permitting ourselves the fun of fantasies, we move from a view of marriage which is less stereotyped to one which is more realistic. Paradoxically, it is also more romantic. Where else can men so easily become heroes and women become queens? And, as I mentioned in a slightly different way: When we feel more like a hero or heroine *on* our feet, we are more likely to feel heroic *off* of them.

Of course, permission to fantasize is only the first step. I think the enjoyment of daydreams requires not only time, experience, and this new perspective, but also, proof that sexual fantasies are harmless. And so, it may be helpful to discuss those conditions under which fantasies tend to be safe in daily living.

Expanding Fantasies II: Safety in Distance

When distance, due to physical or moral barriers, exists between us and the object of our fantasies, it is not only safer to fantasize —it is easier. Why?

To answer this question, we might briefly explore fantasies in three common situations:

1. In private
2. In public
3. In private or public, but when we are alone with someone.

Distance in situations 1 and 2 allows our fantasies to be expanded and enjoyed, but closeness in situation 3 transforms our daydreams into plans and realistic preoccupations. The reason for this transformation should become clear in the following descriptions.

1. *Fantasies in private:* Many daydreams occur when we are sitting home alone. These fantasies may be triggered by looking at picture albums, listening to favorite music, rummaging through old closets or school yearbooks, rereading letters and papers, or simply staring at four walls. There is little danger in this universal pastime. In fact, what could be more harmless than reliving bits and secrets from the past over scrapbooks and snapshots and solitude? Indeed, where could more distance exist between fantasy and reality than at home, alone?

2. *Fantasies in public:* Away from the house, fantasies occur at closer range. And yet, most prove absolutely safe. In public, distance exists between us and the object of our imagination, but it is measured in different ways.

Distance can be measured across the length of crowded rooms: Is it not perfectly harmless to fantasize across the airport lounge or hotel lobby? Across the aisle on buses, trains, or planes? Across the room during coffee breaks and cocktail parties? Or, distance can be symbolized by physical barriers—such as, the desk: Do not teachers and students fantasize on both sides of their respective desks? Do not most people fantasize, at some time, over their desks at work? In libraries? In physicians' offices?

Literally, the distance between us and our daydreams is blocked by people and objects. Figuratively, it is also blocked by moral codes, unwritten rules, professional ethics, and the knowledge that (at least under normal circumstances) fantasies will remain fantasies at school, work, doctors' offices, libraries, airports—in public.

3. *Fantasies in both places—alone with one other person:* A married friend recently confessed: "I'm not going to the office party this Christmas. You have to be on your toes every minute. It's no fun. It's too dangerous." There is a major difference, I think, between the "safety" in office coffee breaks and "danger" in office Christmas parties. Indeed there is a difference between admiring the teacher (or student) across the desk during school and being alone with him; between having a scheduled appointment with the doctor and having an unscheduled drink with him; between noticing the bra-less hitchhiker and picking her up.

In those cases where two people meet face to face, where an inner smile might become an open invitation—fantasies tend to dissolve. Why? Without distance, predictable situations become unpredictable. Fantasies become possible realities. Face to face— in a car, bar, or caught in an elevator with someone special—we may feel excited, aroused, speechless, even mild panic. But we are no longer dealing with fantasies. We are simply too busy dealing with the realistic preoccupations: "What do I say? How do I look? Am I being cool? What happens next?" At such times we are likely to describe our inner world very accurately. We report: "I stopped daydreaming—I came to my senses!"

(Nothing could be closer than two people making love. And yet, fantasies during sexual intercourse may be shut off in similar ways. The need to expand fantasies in bed is an important and complicated subject, one which is explored in Chapter 5.)

Expanding Fantasies III: A Double Life

Most of us enjoy sexual daydreams; we recognize ourselves in this chapter and its examples. Yet, our fantasies still tend to be denied. They just seem too out-of-character with our normal roles during the day. At work, we may exude seriousness and respectability to our colleagues. At home, we may be the model of responsibility to our children. In both places, it may be natural to view our sexual fantasies as alien to such sensible roles.

The problem is that in being so sensible all day, we forget our needs to be a bit wild at night. We lose sight of our need to let loose, let our hair down, and be a little crazy. We neglect such qualities as spontaneity, imagination, childishness, normal eccentricities, and primitive feelings. These are not expressed in most eight-to-five jobs. Indeed, this side of ourselves is difficult to reveal at any hour—at work or home.

One answer is that in developing our fantasy life, we are expressing this part of our personality, at least, mentally. In daydreams, we need not be cool or mature or reasonable. In fact, we can be unreasonable, immature, and uncool. In a word, we can be . . . passionate. And it is in this sense that our fantasy production can be extremely helpful to most of us.

In the end, of course, fantasies are not enough in a good relationship. We need to express ourselves not only in thoughts but in actions. Silly and frivolous actions. Impulsive and unpredictable actions. Wild and primitive actions. But, how do we do so in a respectable marriage? The best answer, I think, is the subject of our next chapter: "Making Love."

5

Making Love: For Whom the Earth Moves

The purpose of this chapter is to focus on what I believe to be the major sexual problem in long-term relationships: The monotony of monogamy. Or, bedroom boredom. I have included two sections on background: "Sexual Prejudices" and "Getting the Facts." One section on boredom, itself: "My Sex Life Is Not Now That Which It Once Was," and seven sections on possible ways to relieve the three- or thirty-year itch: "The Secret Is . . . ," "Variety Is the Spice," "Breaking the Sound Barrier," "Sexual Complaints," "Faking It," "Cleaning the Slate," and "Mastering the Art."

Sexual Prejudices: Sublime and Ridiculous

Sexual attitudes passed down between generations vary from being extremely helpful to equally unhelpful. The following paragraphs from two letters, written by mothers to their eighteen-year-old daughters, provide a study in contrasts. The first letter ends:

". . . Finally, do what you believe is right. You already know my thoughts. Intercourse is still very special and is best reserved for the person you love. But remember, above all, with the right person nothing in this world is better than a good and gratifying sex life . . . "

The second letter also concludes with a thought about intercourse. However, this parent summarizes:

" . . . know that sex is something men want—and women have to do. But don't worry. Intercourse really isn't much worse than going to the bathroom. In fact, I always considered sex—how to put this into words??—well, it's sort of like doing number three . . . "

From these few lines, we are offered a brief glimpse into two mothers' prejudices about lovemaking. It is just such antithetical attitudes as these, I believe, which symbolize the wide range of sexual feelings communicated by parents to their children. To mother number one, sex is fun. To mother number two, it's a function.

It goes without saying that hearing these notions, spoken and unspoken, from infancy to adolescence, a person's feelings about sexuality tend to be deeply rooted and slowly changed. Yet, most people do eventually modify (at least to some extent) their parents' sexual teachings. They do so through a mixture of trial, error, and life experience.

For some men and women, experimenting in bed with a variety of partners proves helpful before marriage. For others, married or not, growth comes through one meaningful relationship—with one particular partner. For still others, they get hung-up at various sexual levels and cannot get "unhung" without some form of outside assistance.

The way an individual moves from parental to personal knowledge about sex is, of course, important. What is more important, however, is a firm belief that although we may be strongly influenced by past prejudices, we need not be strictly committed to them. Whether our parents' view was healthy or unhealthy, we can continue to develop. And as a starting point, whether we are sophisticated or naïve about lovemaking, most of us can further our sexual development by getting helpful information.

Getting the Facts

Today, more people have better access to the sexual facts of life. In many United States cities, at least, there exists an overwhelming number of films, books, magazines, pamphlets, articles, and over-the-counter equipment on the subject. Sex education is now offered through school systems, church groups, university extension courses, and such private agencies as Planned Parenthood. Officially, the pendulum of sexual information has swung 180 degrees.

Or has it? Unofficially, many adolescents and adults remain embarrassed around sexual questions. For various reasons, they lack information in specific areas where they could use help.

For example: A thirty-six-year-old nuclear physicist and his wife became sexually distant after the birth of their third child. In marital therapy, among other revelations, they mentioned an anatomical problem. He confessed: "Frankly, her vagina—this is really hard for me to say—has become big and mushy. I hate to make a pun, but it's a huge problem." Humiliated, she burst into tears and said: "Oh God—I know. Since the last baby, I can hardly feel him inside me."

It seemed that neither husband nor wife, both highly intelligent people, had heard of Kegel exercises.* But, it was also true neither had voiced their specific concerns to a doctor (or each other) until that hour in therapy.

Another well-educated couple believed the husband's difficulty with premature ejaculations was incurable because his instant orgasms characterized their sex life during five years of marriage. Sadly, the couple's only experimentation involved the wife's

---

* Muscles of the vaginal wall are stretched during childbirth. Kegel exercises help return muscles to their original tone. Instructions: "Squeeze or tighten the muscles around the bladder and anal openings as if you are trying to keep the bladder from emptying. Hold these muscles contracted as long as you can. At first this will be difficult, but with practice you can hold them contracted for twenty or thirty seconds. Do this ten times, three times daily." John Miller, M.D., *Childbirth* (New York, Atheneum, 1966) page 148.

lying on her back—like a corpse—so as not to overexcite her husband. Given books, they were surprised, embarrassed, and relieved to find their problem was a common one for which there were many alternative solutions.*

Some post-menopausal women do not know the benefits of estrogens. Nor do some post-myocardial men understand about exercise (to include sex) after a heart attack. Finally, people in their sixties and seventies are commonly reluctant to ask sexual questions. Yet, lovemaking is certainly prevalent among older couples, being more a function of good health and an available partner, than a function of age itself.

Thus, I believe that sexual information can be helpful to people at all ages and all levels of education.† Several books that are excellent for presenting "the facts" in clear, readable, and supportive fashion include:

For Pre- and Early Teens:
> Wardell B. Pomeroy, *Boys and Sex* (New York, Delacorte Press, 1968) and *Girls and Sex* (New York, Delacorte Press, 1969). Both are now available in paperback.
>
> (Note. The abortion information needs to be updated since the late sixties.)

For Older Adolescents and Adults:
> Alex Comfort (editor), *The Joy of Sex* (New York, Crown, 1972).

---

* Simple options for the man involve: (a) ejaculating quickly the first time—then making love a second time more slowly, (b) changing positions: for instance, with his wife on top to minimize his thrusts and stimulation, (c) increasing the length of foreplay before penetration; so that his wife might be brought to a faster climax herself, (d) experimenting with the "squeeze technique" in masturbation—alone or together—where he could practice approaching orgasm, stopping, building up, slowing down, building, slowing, and so forth. For more on the subject, see also Alex Comfort, *The Joy of Sex* (New York, Crown, 1972).

† A concise, complete, and descriptive reading list may be obtained free of charge from the Sex Information and Education Council of the U.S. Write and include a self-addressed, stamped envelope to SIECUS, 1855 Broadway, New York, New York 10023.

For Everyone:
>   Current contraceptive information may be obtained from your
>   physician and is also available free in pamphlet form. It can
>   be secured from your local Planned Parenthood organization
>   or from their national office: Planned Parenthood World
>   Population, 810 Seventh Avenue, New York, New York
>   10019.

Of course, facts alone aren't enough. Many couples who are
experienced and knowledgeable continue to have an unrewarding sex life. They might be extremely well-read about sexuality,
yet all the books in the world don't help in their ability to make
love. One reason for the problem, I think, lies in a person's
false expectations about sexual information. By getting the
facts, men and women naturally expect intercourse to improve.
But since sexual excitement depends so much on individual
taste, the best information about lovemaking ultimately stems
from couples themselves.

To use an analogy of scratching one's back: We might read
in books or see in films that most people enjoy having their back
scratched. And yet, such generalities don't really help. We
can't do a first class job of backscratching without specific
personal instructions: "Down further. Right. Slightly left. Up.
Over a little. That's it. Harder . . . easier . . . there . . . ahhh
. . . perfect!" So, too, couples must develop similar ways to tell
each other what gives them sexual pleasure.

However, before we discuss "what helps" in lovemaking—as
well as how that information might be communicated between
two lovers—let us first briefly touch upon what doesn't help
or the problem of sexual boredom.

"My Sex Life Is Not Now
That Which It Once Was"

From time to time, even in good sexual relationships, lovemaking becomes routine, rigid, and unrewarding. In a word—

boring. To deal directly with sexual boredom, however, often becomes a problem in itself. The following conversation between a successful suburban woman and her psychiatrist illustrates one variation on a common complaint.

Mrs. H: Does everyone feel trapped in their marriage at certain times? Lately, I just want to escape from the house, the kids, my husband, the job . . . you name it. I've begun to think: "I'm stuck" and "Is this the way my life is always going to be?" Quite honestly, I think something's very wrong with me. Wrong because I've also started to have distressing thoughts about an old friend.

Dr. I: By "thoughts," you mean sexual fantasies about him?

Mrs. H: Thoughts, fantasies, daydreams, nightmares, whatever you want to call them. It must be related to what's happening at home.

Dr. I: What's happening?

Mrs. H: Sexually . . . very little. In fact, our lovemaking is almost nil. My husband's so exhausted that we're having sex three or four times a month. (It used to be several times a week.) Our timing in bed is terribly off; he's too quick—while I'm having the opposite trouble. Now, I have problems getting aroused. When I ask my husband to slow down, he'll dutifully kiss my breasts or rub my clitoris for an extra five minutes. But that doesn't really help. I start to blame him and then remember, "Here I am lying passively, afraid to touch him. Afraid he'll come faster if I move. So, sex must be as boring for him as for me." Anyway, our sex life has become some stereotyped ritual without any real passion or even pleasure. It's an act we perform out of duty. Like, we do "it" each Saturday night. Or every-other-Wednesday. It's horrible.

Dr. I: Have you discussed the problem with your husband?

Mrs. H: Not really. He's so tired these days. And besides, where do I begin?

Specifics aside, the woman's plight is one frequently heard after several years of marriage. Frequently, I think, because the result is such a demoralizing cycle: (In brief, less energy ⟶ less lovemaking ⟶ worse timing ⟶ worse sex ⟶ even less energy and desire ⟶ even less sex ⟶ creating more distance ⟶ making it harder to talk and interrupt the cycle . . .) The wife is right: "Where do I begin?"

Bedroom boredom: hopeless sign or helpful signal?

One starting point is our recognizing a basic fact of married life. Periods of sexual boredom are inevitable in long-term relationships. Living with one person for two, or twenty, years, we cannot hope to maintain constantly high levels of sexual tension and excitement. From time to time, all of us feel "Oh Lord, not tonight," or "Oh no, I'm simply too tired (again)." The reality is that sexual doldrums, like arguments, are a predictable part of marriage. Yet boredom, like anger, can also paradoxically signal a time for closeness, not more distance in a good relationship.

Our first problem, however, is to recognize the signal. Does "I'm feeling trapped" mean, in fact, "My sex life has become boring?" Does "I'm fantasizing more" imply "Our lovemaking is getting rigid, routine, and unrewarding?" Do our escape and erotic fantasies really serve as the tip of a sexual iceberg?

If so, our feeling "trapped" or "stuck" or "hopeless" becomes an early warning sign of what isn't happening at home. Such signals, in turn, may help us confront the recurring problem of boredom in bed. Of course, "helpful signal" and "confront the problem" imply some type of positive action. Let us ask: What kind of action? Practically speaking, what helps us to alleviate our sexual boredom after we recognize it?

The Secret Is . . .

In general, most of us look for "the" answer to solve our problems. "All I really need is . . . more money." Or, "My life would dramatically change with . . . a new job . . . bigger home . . . better security."

In particular, we also look for single answers to resolve our problems in bed. No one who watches television commercials or reads magazine advertisements could fail to recognize the obvious exploitation of our search for sexual help. If only we: take daily supplements of iron and vitamins; gargle with mouthwash; spray with deodorants; brush with sexy toothpaste; wear the right bra; drive the new car—magically, with these new products . . . comes new life.

So, too, there's new life in bed, if only we use the latest secret formula. From Vitamin E to Kamasutra oil, from whipped cream on nuts to strawberry douches, the message is clear: Our sexual prayers could be answered with a simple lotion, potion, oil, or pill.

More traditionally, "the" key to lovemaking lies in "technique." Sexual success depends upon a couple's mastering various locations and positions. Yet, as a bewildered young man said after reading one marriage manual: "I know that penis goes into vagina. But, in some of those positions, how the heck do you slip left thigh into right elbow?"

Another person believed the secret was "orgasms." In this man's view, revealed in marital counseling, sex wasn't the problem in their marriage. The fact was that he and his wife usually did achieve orgasm; except his wife then interrupted to say their lovemaking hadn't varied one whit in three years. Even with climaxes, she found their sex life incredibly dull.

Her orgasms were, as she later put it, "Nice—but certainly not the whole story."

My own feeling is that focusing on climaxes or technique or gimmicks only leads to further distortions and false expectations. Our search continues for magic formulas and secret doors. In short, going from newest product to latest prescription, we mistakenly believe there does exist a single key to unlock that special door—behind which lie all the answers.*

Sexual intimacy: locked door or jig-saw puzzle?

To open locked doors, the secret is to find the right key. But, to solve sexual problems, not unlike jig-saw puzzles, the secret is . . . there is no secret.

Might not lovemaking more accurately be likened to a complex puzzle? The complete picture being the sum of its pieces, the blending together of its various parts: variety, technique, information, experience, experimentation, practice, privacy, signals, fantasies, hormones, craziness, trust, tenderness, good health, good feelings. . . . The names don't really matter. Nor does the order or style in which they fit into place. What does matter is a basic reality: The more pieces that fit, the more complete the final picture. And, the more complete the picture, the easier for us to see what's missing from it.

For most of us, something's always missing. During some periods, we can't find time and energy. During other periods, we lack the necessary chemistry. At other times, we have sex in predictable ways leaving out the elements of surprise and spontaneity.

Yet, elements which are lost one year may be found the next year, and vice versa. Parts of the sexual puzzle that fit yester-

---

* Typical of this viewpoint was the final remark in an article, "All About the New Sex Therapies," *Newsweek* (November 27, 1972), pages 65 to 72. Concluding the article was the following quote about sexual performance: "It's like learning to ride a bicycle, once you get the hang of it, you never forget."

day, don't fit today. Indeed, a couple's love life is seldom now
that which it once was. The picture is always changing.

Variety Is the Spice

I mentioned under "Sexual Fantasies" that when a person's
daily life is relatively respectable, his night life becomes the
perfect place to be a little wild. Let loose. Have fun. Go safely
crazy. Lovemaking, I implied, can offer two people a helpful balance to their normal eight-to-five routine. Varied sex
can provide much of what the day lacks.

Variety in bed, however, is not simply a matter of having
intercourse in odd places and off-beat positions. In fact, to vary
lovemaking, for its own sake, can become yet another boring
ritual. To paraphrase a Hollywood "hero" in the film *Carnal
Knowledge:* "We've had sex in the bathtub, shower, living room,
and den. We've tried all the positions. We've alternated mornings, afternoons, and nights. We've done everything in the books.
And yet, I'm so fucking bored I'm going nuts."

In this case, the hero's problem lies in the misconception that
sexual variety can be learned from books. I say "misconception"
because to read about lovemaking is, again, similar to reading
about backscratching. In general, it may be helpful to learn about
erotic and new ways to rub one's back, yet ultimately, kinds of
scratches are dictated by types of internal itches. The location
and intensity of which are constantly changing.

So, too, with sexual scratching. It is also determined by internal needs and feelings, which change from year to year, month
to month, day to day. As such, sexual variety is most meaningful
when it accurately reflects what a person feels in bed this week,
this night . . . this moment.

Most of us, however, cannot predict our feelings before we
make love. The Friday night when "I'm too tired" may prove a
delightful surprise; the Sunday alone together, "we'll spend in
bed," a mild disappointment. We cannot predict the nights we'll

feel more aggressive and passionate versus those nights we'll feel more submissive and passive during intercourse. We cannot predict if we'll be more active with our lips—kissing, biting, licking, and sucking. We can't predict not only about our hands—touching, holding, grabbing, scratching—but which combination of so-called "erogenous zones" our tongue and fingers will arouse on any particular night: ears, lips, neck, breasts, nipples, shoulder, back, buttocks, thighs, penis, clitoris, vagina. There's no "right place" or "right time." We cannot predict positions: face to face, sitting, kneeling, standing, in bed or out of it. We cannot predict when our spontaneous desires will be triggered by our lover's spontaneous reactions. We cannot predict rhythm: times to speed up or slow down; move or lie quietly; times to wait or build quickly, thrust hard and explode. We cannot predict our signals: Do we communicate with words, touch, moans, groans, heavy breathing, or soft whispering? Or, do we remain silent in hopes that our lover will somehow guess our inner needs? We cannot predict our feelings during the foreplay, the climax, the aftermath. Our reactions vary from one moment to the next: passion, boredom, reality, and fantasy merge and clash without warning. Small wonder that film hero's premeditated attempts to have sex "in the bathtub" and "on the floor" missed the point.

Whereas sexual formulas in books, magazines, or movies may trigger our imagination, they can also become a substitute for it. They can offer someone else's fantasies for our own; prescribed variety for the spontaneous kind; gymnastics for the subtleties and nuances of lovemaking.

Varied sex truly comes from inner needs which are unpredictable and unconscious. We don't say to ourselves: "I'm feeling more sadistic tonight. I want to hurt you." Or: "I'm feeling more childish and dependent this week—I want to bite, suck, and be held more than usual." On the contrary, such feelings come and go without logic or design. They bubble up with inspiration, not calculation. They flow from an inner wellspring,

not an outer source. And it becomes crucial in long-term relationships that we learn to tap that wellspring.* In short, that
we recognize the kingdom of sexual variety dwells within us.

Breaking the Sound Barrier

As "variety" implies more than "on the floor," so too, breaking
the sound barrier during lovemaking implies more than fifteen
minutes of silence followed by "I love you" or "Are you okay?"
or more bluntly, "Did 'ja cum?" Let me repeat: In bed, couples
must help each other in the same way that one person directs
another to scratch his back. There is no substitute for clear
instructions, verbal or nonverbal, which mean "left . . . down
. . . harder . . . there . . . ah, perfect."

Of course, most of us find it hard to be so direct about our
sexual needs. Instead, we develop familiar codes to send sexual
messages. For instance, most of us have indirect ways to announce: "No sex tonight." As one wife said, "When my husband
hints about making love in the evening, I usually answer: 'I'm
pretty pooped,' which translates: 'Test me and see what happens.' Or, 'I'm exhausted. I'm going to bed before I fall asleep
on the couch,' which means: 'Not tonight.'"

One husband who was married thirteen years revealed:
"Whenever my wife pats my chest five to six times before lights
out, she's telling me: 'Wait until tomorrow.' On my part, I
frequently say, 'Why don't you go to sleep, love? Maybe I'll
stay up and read or catch the late show.'"

Such harmless charades before lovemaking are familiar to

* Some of the conscious reasons for shutting off our inner feelings and
fantasies were discussed in Chapter 4. For example, preoccupations during
intercourse such as: Did I pay that bill? Take my pill? Will the neighbors
hear? Will the kids? Can I last? Will I make it? Can my back take it? Needless to conclude, such distractions do not help us tap our reservoir of various
sexual feelings. (Many ideas in this section and on page 67 are extensions
of thoughts presented by Ralph R. Greenson, M.D., in a talk entitled: "Sex
Without Passion," delivered at University of California Medical Center, San
Francisco, on March 27, 1966.)

all of us. During lovemaking, however, two people may be reluctant to signal each other, directly or indirectly, for limitless reasons: embarrassment, fear, habit, lack of practice, or being "lost for words." And yet, it is not helpful to make love in silence week after week, month after month. Not only do silent nights become another deadly routine, but they also force lovers to make assumptions about their partner's inner feelings. And those feelings, as I mentioned in the last section, are constantly changing.

Therefore, hard as it is, couples must develop a working system of signals to insure that today's lovemaking is not based on yesterday's assumptions. To put it another way: If sex is not to become rigid and boring, couples must find ways to share how they feel (and what they need) this month, this week, this night.

Again, the question: Where to begin?

Signals: familiar or foreign language?

In broad terms, I think it is important to start by expressing the *positive* feelings that bubble up during lovemaking. In specific terms, it is most helpful for couples to share expressions of pleasure, such as:

> "It's good to feel so close."
> "You give me everything."
> "My wonderful woman."
> "My big bull."
> "I love you."
> "I need you."

If genuinely felt, such words help to create a warm, loving, and safe atmosphere. Safety, in turn, allows couples to teach each other about their immediate sexual needs without fear of laughter or humiliation. In a safe climate the woman, for example, can better help the man learn about her inner feelings. She can tell him (among other things):

"Wait. Hold me. Let's talk for a few minutes before we start."
"Kiss my neck."
"Lower."
"Touch me."
"Be gentle."
"Go deeper."
"Come inside of me . . . can you wait?"

Here, the wife's simple instructions avoid embarrassing or graphic words. They direct her husband without offense and, in the process, show him ways to express his own feelings.

"I don't know if I can wait . . . "
"Stop for a minute."
"Roll over."
"Come on top of me."
"Keep it up."
"Good . . . go . . . ah . . . "

In addition, two people have an infinite variety of nonverbal signals—kissing, biting, sucking, holding, moving, moaning, breathing—to guide the tempo of lovemaking. For most people: Actions can speak softer than words.

A woman's rolling over on her stomach can be a more delicate communication than saying: "Come in from behind me."

Moving her lover's lips can be more pleasing than gagging on the words "breasts" or "nipples" or "clitoris."

A man's shifting his wife's hand from upper thigh to penis avoids similar difficulties with "masturbate." As does shifting her head preclude the mention of "blow" or "suck" or "go down" or even "kiss me."

To repeat my prejudice: Such signals cannot be learned from reading books or watching films. They cannot be gleaned from sex-education instruction, regardless of how clear the information. They must be learned from having sex with the person we love.

Why?

Because signals, overt or covert, involve a special language based upon *our inner feelings* in bed *at the moment.* ("Hold me" . . . "Stop" . . . "Roll over" . . . "Climb on top" . . .) These are external manifestations of our internal needs. "Hold me. Let's talk" expresses a woman's reluctance to start making love, her need to relax or to be reassured. "Stop for a minute" can imply that a man's climaxing too quickly, and he wants to delay it. A wife's signaling the husband to come in from behind her implies a spontaneous feeling of what she'd enjoy . . . and how she'd enjoy it.

As we learn to reveal such feelings, we learn to speak a new language. A language we can master only through persistent effort and frequent mistakes . . . over many years of constant practice.

Sexual Complaints

Occasionally, husbands and wives discuss in a psychiatric office sexual complaints they are unable to discuss at home. In some cases, the person may recognize his inner feelings, but he can't signal them to a loved one. For example, I have heard women complain:

"My husband works on construction projects all day, and he'll often forget to bathe at night. The problem is that I know of no tactful way, especially just before making love, to announce that his smell bothers me."

"When my husband returns from business trips, he expects me to instantly 'turn-on' in bed. Yet, I need to talk; enjoy a shower together; be held before intercourse; stop in the middle of it—I need to go slow. My husband has never understood the reasons for my coolness after those trips. And I've never explained these needs to him. They seem so obvious to me."

"My husband has one terribly annoying habit during sex. For the two years of our marriage, I've had to take his penis in hand—literally—and insert it before we make love. Honestly, I'm ashamed to admit that something so small bothers me so much. But if I'm embarrassed to tell you about it, how am I ever going to tell him?"

I have heard men complain:

"My wife simply isn't passionate in bed. Actually, she can have orgasms, but she just lies passively during sex. I've had one affaire in fifteen years and the only difference between that girl and my wife was oral sex. (Which I liked.) Yet, realistically, how do I ask my wife to go down on me? She'd absolutely die."

"My wife's an attractive person. But, unfortunately, she wears no make-up and dresses like a girl scout. We go in 'hip' circles so, theoretically, clothes and cosmetics shouldn't matter to me. I'm supposed to be happy with her 'natural look.' But, hell, I want my wife to look good when we go to friends' homes. I want to be proud of her when we go out to restaurants. Now you tell me: What can I say?"

At this point, let us ask: Why do some married couples share these charged feelings with a psychiatrist, but not with each other? Indeed, why do most of us have trouble discussing sexual complaints with the person we love?

One reason lies in the fact that many of our sexual feelings and fantasies imply criticism of our husband or wife. Should we announce our hidden feelings about lovemaking ("go slower" . . . "go lower" . . .), our partner hears not only "Something's wrong with our sex life," but more painfully, "Something's wrong with me." And that conclusion has unpleasant repercussions. Hearing sexual complaints, most of us react with silent anger ("Go to hell"), hurt ("Never again will I try . . ."), indignation ("Who are you to criticize?"), and insecurity ("What else is wrong with me?"). Thus, one hurdle between our sexual ideas and their announcement is a basic dilemma: How to put critical thoughts into kind words? How to suggest changes in bed without hurting the other person?

If a method exists for husbands and wives to share their critical feelings without inflicting some pain, I don't know it. The fact is that criticism hurts. Especially sexual criticism. And yet, there is no substitute for direct talk if couples hope to learn from their sexual mistakes. In other words: Two lovers must teach each other not only what helps, but what doesn't help before, during, and after intercourse. Painful or not, how else can sex improve and relationships grow?

In voicing sexual complaints, however, we need not open extensive wounds. Anticipating some hurt, we can pick an evening to complain when we feel relaxed and close, instead of angry, tense, and distant. A night when we have the courage to speak in detail rather than generalities. A time when our partner can *hear* our criticism—as well as be stung by it.

At such moments, it helps for two people to trust each other. Trust, because we must know that our sexual criticism will not provoke lasting personal counterattacks. We must believe that our lover's defensiveness will eventually turn into understanding; anger into action; hurt into a need to please us.

It is our needing to please each other, I believe, which ultimately creates the necessary atmosphere not only to recognize sexual feelings (positive or negative), but to express them.

"Faking It" and "The Need to Please"

Let us now ask the opposite question: Do conditions arise when two lovers should not express their inner feelings? Or, putting it another way: Should couples express what isn't felt during sex?

To answer these questions, I interviewed a couple, married fourteen years, who described an excellent sex life together. Indeed, they claimed "Our lovemaking gets better every year." Asked in separate interviews about performing in bed, husband and wife shared a common viewpoint. To this couple at least, their definition of "faking it" as "needing to please" seemed not only accurate, but helpful. The following excerpts summarize their comments:

Confessions of a sexually satisfied husband

"I've read in books that most women fake orgasms during sex and that implies a bad marriage. I disagree. My wife undoubtedly pretends from time to time. Not only don't I know, but I don't really care. The important part is feeling her active enjoyment, real or imagined. It must satisfy some primitive need in me. The satisfaction of believing I'm a good lover, a potent lover, a sensitive lover—possibly the best lover in the world. That's satisfaction.

"Yet, to give satisfaction, my wife has to respond with passion instead of passivity when I have a climax. But how can she be passionate every time? How can I? Can anyone?

"The truth is: I also fake it. Maybe I'm unique—men don't talk about this subject. Or, at least I've never heard anyone mention husbands as actors. Still, on rare occasions, I honestly (or dishonestly) perform in bed. For instance: My wife's about to have an orgasm—and I'm not. When she does reach her climax, I try not to keep flailing away in the midst of her final convulsion. Here's the moment to grab and hold on. To give a last thrust. To fake my own seizure. I know that it's artificial to stop when I'm really throbbing inside her, but I want to please her as much as . . . God knows . . . she pleases me. Besides, my turn comes next.

"I've also learned to pretend in the opposite situation: When I can't last, when I'm too fast. After my climax, I'm satisfied, but it is she who now continues to throb around me. I am perhaps luckier than some men at such times. Lucky, when I'm rested, because my erection remains hard enough for my wife to climb on top and 'use me.' Within a few minutes in that position, she can usually reach her own orgasm.

"My performance at those moments doesn't come naturally. It is very difficult, I think, for men to show honest interest after an orgasm. My natural inclination after coming is to roll over, drift in a million directions, and fall into a deep sleep. It is hard to stay interested, to move, to wait for her climax. Yet, actor or not, I know this would-be second-coming helps my wife. On these nights, sex is better for her. And therefore, it's better for me."

Confessions of a sexually satisfied wife

"Faking it is an old story for me. Before meeting my husband, I did have relations with several men and found sex not only pleasant, but exciting. Although I never had an orgasm, my faking a climax seemed the natural way to end intercourse.

"After marriage, I started having orgasms and there followed two years of very beautiful lovemaking. However, I then became pregnant. For almost nine months, I lost all interest in sex. But, during that period, I knew it was terribly important to my husband's self-esteem to feel that he excited me. So, I again began to fake it. I soon learned that the option of faking it to please my husband removed any worries I had about my performance. Now, having orgasms or faking them, I do enjoy the 'connected' feeling of close lovemaking. And my husband does enjoy me. But don't misunderstand. Faking it, I think, is still a substitute for the real thing.

"How typical is my situation? I just don't know. In the past fourteen years, only two lady friends have discussed this specific problem with me. And then, only because they were so miserable.

"One friend confided that during the nursing of her first child, she had no sexual interest. Zero. Not only was she concerned about it, but her husband—who had been very understanding during the pregnancy—was near panic. My suggestion that she fake it, to relieve the pressure on everyone, shocked her. She felt that any performance on her part would be dishonest and unreal.

"The other friend complained bitterly about her sex life after one year of marriage. (She had three or four premarital experiences, but her husband had been a virgin before their meeting.) So, to build his confidence, my friend 'performed' in bed. Unfortunately, the husband subsequently assumed that he was a great lover and never did vary his adolescent style of lovemaking during the whole twelve months. What could she do?

"Obviously, should the concept of faking it be taken literally in either extreme—of total honesty or total dishonesty—it becomes unhelpful. For me, faking it is just one of many helpful ways to please my husband."

Cleaning the Slate

Of course, two lovers don't always feel like faking it or pleasing each other. Although the following point may seem obvious, it does warrant brief mention before the chapter's conclusion: As preoccupations during sex interfere with tuning into feelings and fantasies; so too, a couple's anger or hurt before sex interferes with their wanting to please the other person. It is difficult to enjoy lovemaking with favorite four-letter words on the tip of one's tongue. Or, with tears in one's eyes. Maybe this is one reason why such house rules as "Never Go To Bed Mad" become so crucial in good sexual relationships.

Whereas the husband, angry or depressed at bedtime, might still be able to enjoy quickies—his wife cannot. She needs to feel close and connected to her man before intercourse. She must have some resolution of their hidden agendas, the under-

lying problems between her and her husband. Therefore, especially for the woman, private hurts must be shared at night.
Whether such negative feelings are realistic or unrealistic
doesn't really matter. What does matter, I believe, is that
couples do everything possible to clean their inner slate before
making love.

Mastering the Art

How does the logical approach of this chapter help two people
in something as illogical, irrational, and intuitive as good lovemaking?

"Getting the facts" certainly doesn't arouse images of passionate or primitive sex. Tuning into sensual feelings—this
week, this night, this moment—sounds more like hard work
than romantic love. Couples' exchanging signals smacks more
of doing business than giving pleasure. Offering criticism and
resolving arguments seems neither delicious nor fun. Learning
to "fake-it" neither impulsive nor inspirational. So, let us again
question: How does two lovers' mastery of these practical fundamentals relate to the chemistry and magic of spontaneous
sexuality?

It does so in ways similar to two dancers who can electrify
audiences with their brilliant spontaneity and improvisation.
The Nureyevs and Fonteyns who devote lifetimes to mastering fundamentals, so that they can burst forth and go wild
at any given moment. Indeed, it is only after years of such
practice that any artist can forget the fundamentals and lose
himself in his art. So too, I think two lovers' uninhibited productions in bed are based upon the same principle. In short,
couples must first master the details of sex before they can
discard them.

Later, when our preoccupations about details are forgotten,
reality fades. Sexual feelings and fantasies bubble up. Hormones
flow and signals follow. At those moments we are totally free

to let loose and lose control. We are capable of bursting forth, going wild. Mastered fundamentals have become the spring-board to spontaneous performances. And, with spontaneity and freedom, our lovemaking becomes so personal, so intense, so unpredictable that we indeed begin to dissolve into that other experience . . . other person . . . other world. Or, in Heming-way's simple and famous lines in *For Whom the Bell Tolls* we

". . . feel as though I wanted to die when I am loving thee."
"Oh," she said, "I die each time. Do you not die?"
"No. Almost. But did thee feel the earth move?"
"Yes, as I died . . . "

6

Values: Time As Well As Money

Has not the word come to you
that the flower is reigning in
splendour among thorns?
Wake, oh awaken! Let not the
time pass in vain!
—RABINDRANATH TAGORE

Micawber's Rule: The Line
Between Happiness and Misery

One problem with money is there's seldom enough of it. Regardless of a family's income, monthly bills often exceed the monthly paycheck—with unhappy results. The story is not a new one. To paraphrase Mr. Micawber's lament to the young hero in *David Copperfield:* "You know, income twenty pounds, expenditure nineteen pounds—result: happiness. Income twenty pounds, expenditure twenty-one pounds—result: misery." And thus, Micawber concludes: "The blossom is blighted, the leaf is withered, the God of day goes down upon the dreary scene, and in short you are forever floored. As I am."

There exist several modern translations of Charles Dickens' classic observation. The popular expressions for our 20/21 financial vision and monthly miseries are numerous:

"I have to moonlight."

"Why else am I in the rat race?"

"I'm on a treadmill (to oblivion and to pay off my creditors)."

"Best I keep my nose pressed firmly to the grindstone, lest our debts spin wildly out of control."

In many homes, a pair's frustration is symbolized by their checkbook's being out-of-balance by month's end . . . regardless of income! This last point is underscored in the following budgets:

A single secretary who earns $500 per month:

Taxes	$ 50
Housing	$180
Food and Drink	$100
Car	$ 50
Insurance	$ 30
Cleaning and Clothes	$ 30
Fun and Games	$ 40
Other (Medical, Dental, Cosmetics, etc.)	$ 70
Total Expenses	$550

A public accountant who earns $1700 per month:

Taxes	$ 350
Housing	$ 400
Food and Drink	$ 250
Insurance	$ 150
Investments	$ 100
Clothes, etc.	$ 100
Fun and Games	$ 100
Children	$ 100
Cars (2)	$ 150
Other (Medical, Dental, Furniture, Appliances, etc.)	$ 150
Total Expenses	$1850

A dentist who earns $5000 per month:

Taxes	$1300

Housing	$ 800
Food and Drink	$ 500
Insurance	$ 500
Investments	$ 500
Fun and Games	$ 500
Children	$ 250
Cars (3)	$ 400
Other	$ 500
Total Expenses	$5250

A common denominator exists in this range of budgets beyond Micawber's rule. Not only is money a preoccupation which concerns most of us. But also, and it comes as no surprise, we often assume that many of our problems could be solved with more money: An extra $15 per week for the secretary; an extra $200 per month for the C.P.A.; $6,000 per year for the D.D.S. At one level, more money would be useful and this assumption is correct. Yet, at another level and from these examples, it should also be clear that our wishful thinking can prove to be faulty. Commonly, the more we earn, the more we spend. Result: The more we need to earn. Such dilemmas can become vicious cycles which tend to raise havoc in our sexual relationships.

Whereas some financial problems can be resolved in ways other than seeking extra income (see "Simplify," page 96), it might be helpful at this point to describe another false assumption related to a couple's pattern of spending. Not of money, but of time.

Great Expectations: Tomorrow and Tomorrow and Tomorrow

Upon being discharged from the Army, a young soldier hoped to write the Great American Novel. So, he returned to his hometown in Indiana and started the book. After three months, however, the would-be novelist bogged down in the second chapter. He thought: "The Midwest is just too provincial for me. It's too straight, too conservative, too dull, deadendsville for new writers." So, he caught the Greyhound bus and left for New York City. After three months, again, the ex-soldier continued to struggle with Chapter Two. He thought: "I can't write here. New York is too dirty, noisy, chaotic, impersonal, and dangerous. Small wonder there's been no progress." Subsequently, he bought a ticket to California and rode the bus to Hollywood. Predictably, he soon discovered that Los Angeles was too plastic, too smoggy, too ugly, and too lonely to do any good writing. Looking back, the young man concluded: "Wow! What a year. The only place I was ever really happy was riding on that damn bus."

Most of us have a personalized version of our own bus ride into the future. Most of us have lived between stopovers with a common rationalization: "Tomorrow—it will be better." And, indeed, is this not part of the human condition? At some point, do not most of us think:

"When I'm finished with school, it will be better."
"When I'm finally married . . . "
"When the wedding's over . . . "
"When we move into our own apartment . . . "
"When we move out of the apartment into a house . . . "
"When children come . . . "
"When the kids grow (and go) . . . "
"When I have tenure, seniority, that next promotion . . ."
"When I retire . . . "

Paradoxically, after the person is graduated from high school or college, he may later view those years as "the good old days." After marriage, he may confide to single friends, "Boy, are you lucky." After becoming a homeowner, he may find life was cheaper in an apartment. After children, life may have been simpler without them.

Therefore, a variation on the theme: "It *will be* better," is the refrain: "It *was* better." Not only do people look forward with great expectations, but they look backward with great nostalgia.

(Or, as the White Queen tells Alice in Lewis Carroll's *Through the Looking Glass:* "The rule is, jam tomorrow and jam yesterday, but never jam *today.*") The problem is that in living so oriented to tomorrow and yesterday, we tend to neglect today. We neglect the moment. Work is described in such phrases as: "I look forward to coffee breaks" . . . "I can't wait for lunch" . . . "I killed a few hours" or "held-on" or "watched the clock" until quitting time. As we all know: Many jobs become one big battle against the clock. (Meanwhile, folks who remain at home understandably mark time by "getting through" various phases of daily chores: washing dishes, cleaning house, shopping, picking up kids, preparing meals.)

With the result that by day's end many people find it hard to shift gears. Thus, after five o'clock, husbands and wives often continue to "make it through" the commute hour, children's hour, dinner hour, and evening itself. By six, their resistance is low and addiction high to nightly cocktails or evening television. They come to bed like two empty vessels, both in desperate need of refilling. But they collapse at night, totally exhausted. Their style of filling time—or, in some ways, killing it—is an exhausting way to live.

Yet, the fact is that most jobs are repetitious; household chores are monotonous; children are draining. Realistically, most jobs and housework and children do exhaust us. So, what alternatives exist for people to keep from killing time in daily jobs and weekly routines? One alternative begins with an oft quoted, recently popularized line of Mao Tse-tung:

"Seize the day!"

Since our future and past is the sum total of each day—our lives are only as good as each "today." We become tomorrow what we are today. And recognition of that fact becomes a crucial starting point. Here, the assumption is not "It will be better," or "It was better." It is not that "Time is money." But rather: "Time is life."

The purpose of this chapter is to discuss two basic questions: (1) How to increase the free time in a person's day, and (2) How to improve its quality in a couple's life.

Simplify

Beware of all enterprises that require new clothes.
—HENRY DAVID THOREAU

A teacher and friend once remarked: "All of my life I asked: 'What do I need?' Suddenly, I began to ask: 'What *don't* I need?' and I've been happier ever since."

One path to free time lies in the direction of simplification. That path, however, is often cluttered with things. Literally. Instead of working hard and playing hard, many families in the United States work hard and spend hard. Spending, in turn, can lead to a previously described cycle: Earn ⟶ spend ⟶ earn more ⟶ work more ⟶ spend more. Consequently, regardless of income, there's never enough—time or money.

A problem for many families caught in this life style is that in spite of their consumption, they feel empty and unsatisfied. Their work/spend habits do not bring pleasure, nor do they bring nonmaterial rewards. And we might ask: Why?

Most people, I believe, do not really want such things as cars with more horsepower, stereo with higher fidelity, vacuum cleaners with eight attachments, or even sex books with forty-seven of someone else's favorite positions. Because people do not truly want such things may be one reason why they can never buy enough of them. They are merely substitutes. Substitutes for what we really do need and cannot buy in the marketplace: A sense of self-confidence and self-respect. A sense of purpose and direction. A feeling of companionship, closeness, and love. Since we cannot buy these basics, we can never feel totally satisfied buying the substitutes.* We remain

* In a different context, Eric Hoffer made this observation in *The Ordeal of Change* (New York, Harper & Row, 1964), page 4.

somewhat empty; and thus, we consume more, and more, and more.

Here, let us ask: How might we change our assumption from "What more *do* I need?" to "What *don't* I need?"

I think we can begin on this road to simplification by:

1. Getting away: Perspective on material needs becomes clearer with distance. A person can view his daily life in more objective terms during a fishing trip, camping trip, weekend retreat, or summer vacation. For example, simplification becomes easier in mountain or seashore cabins where one requires little more than food and shelter to be perfectly happy.

"We don't need new carpets" may be obvious when a pair is snug as bugs (without rugs) in a mountain hide-a-way. "We don't need a frost-free refrigerator" may also be obvious when couples are delighted just to have an ordinary ice-box in their rustic summer rental. "We don't need a larger home" may be apparent when two people can unwind in a motel room or camper. Relaxation being more a function of distance from their old place than of size in their new one.

2. Putting "things" off: It is also helpful to put off for tomorrow what we might buy today. This advice, of course, is easier said than done. We know that deficit spending is an attractive way of life in today's world. Credit cards, charge accounts, lay-away plans, nothing down, fly now—pay later . . . only make it harder to curb our appetite for things.

And yet, most purchases can be delayed. We can defer many things "I need" for several days, weeks, or months. In fact, when we can procrastinate for a short time (living without "it"), our reaction is frequently one of amazement that we wanted the item so badly in the first place. Such delaying tactics are most helpful in taking the impulse out of buying.

3. Support in saying "no": Rejecting conveniences does not happen without inconveniences. Saying "no" to a second car, for instance, requires that someone must walk, ride the bus, pedal a bicycle, depend upon friends. Such minor "sacrifices" can prove impossible without the mutual cooperation of two people. Both must want a less cluttered life. Thus, simplification involves not only one person's saying "later" or "no," but the other person's supporting him. (Be it in rejecting a second car or in resisting daily advertisements, accumulations, invitations, and seductions of every sort.) Again, success depends upon support; and simplification always takes two people.

If these three measures prove helpful, a family can begin to save money in cases where they normally might spend it. Doing without a second car, in turn, may lead to doing without a second job, as moonlighting tends to become unnecessary with a reduced standard of living. In these ways, a pair can slowly move toward the goal of less complicated living and the bonus of more free time.

That bonus, however, can also be frightening.

Fears of Free Time

It is important to realize that the prospect of free time causes acute anxiety in many people.* Should an individual run at seventy miles per hour during his day, fears of slowing down at night (over weekends) are quite natural. There are numerous examples to describe this phenomenon. A West Coast law firm reached an economic level of success which allowed each partner to take a six months' leave of absence every five years, without any cut in salary. Faced with half a year of unstructured time, however, nine out of ten partners voted *against* going on their own sabbaticals.

Many people consider two-week vacations in similar terms. Working hard all year, they know (and dread) the painful process of unwinding during their annual "rest." Many couples face Sundays with this anxiety. Going in high gear six days,

* For a classic study of this problem, see Erich Fromm, *Escape From Freedom* (New York: Holt, Rinehart & Winston, 1941).

they can't suddenly shift into neutral on the seventh without feeling a bit lost.

These reactions can be less distressing, I think, when viewed as predictable side effects of moving from structured to unstructured time. Expecting some anxiety in that transition may help a person in the early stages of weekends, vacations, or even sabbaticals. Ultimately, of course, such anxiety is lowered when an individual truly believes: "I will be able to shift gears, slow down, relax, and use free time to enjoy myself. Indeed, time *is* life."

But how do we translate such abstract clichés into concrete actions? How do we begin looking forward to our free time?

The Million-Dollar Question

One starting point could be our answer to the mythical question: "What if I suddenly inherited a million dollars?"

To struggle with an imaginary inheritance, we must resolve two basic issues: First, "What to buy?" and second, "What to do?" For most of us, the solution to the first problem is relatively clear. To become a millionaire would be synonymous with a new house, appliances, furniture, swimming pool, cars, clothes, travel, investments. . . . Our list of material needs bubbles up spontaneously and it is easily described. Yet, beyond "How would I spend the money?" lies the harder question: "How would I spend my time?" Honest answers to this dilemma come, I think, neither easily nor spontaneously. Indeed, our first response may be "How I *wouldn't* spend the time."

Given a million dollars, for example, we may know that "I wouldn't continue in the rat race." At work, we'd love to tell our boss in which precise anatomical location to shove the bleeping job. At home, we'd love to leave our mythical maid with the chaos and confusion. In both cases, we'd like to use that money to escape. But we must ask: Escape to where? And, to what?

Positive answers to these simple questions are often unclear for years. Time and effort are clearly necessary in the redefinition of both present and future goals. Once defined, however, these answers can help improve the quality of our lives. On either a part-time or full-time basis.

Million or not, some people who answer this question must then pursue their newly defined goals as a way of life. They pursue their impossible dream as a full-time job. For example:

An English haberdasher's son, age twenty-three, rejected his father's business and successfully wrote novels in the Caribbean Islands.

A black Ph.D. from Yale, age twenty-eight, resigned his teaching post to work in a Boston ghetto.

A State Department career officer, age thirty, quit and returned to the university for a graduate degree in art history.

A high school principal, age forty, dropped out to start his own corporation in Europe.

An I.B.M. executive, age fifty-five, retired ten years early to work for a conservation organization.

A former salami-casing salesman, age thirty-five, ran that organization.

In many families, a person's financial situation does not allow for these romantic and radical changes. Few men see themselves doing what they "really" want to do, full-time, yet still earn their living and maintain their life-style; and few women could totally drop out from their responsibilities at work or home.

As a result, answers to the original question are more realistically implemented on a part-time basis. For most people, experiments with free time must begin during evenings, weekends, and vacations. Here, a person can start doing today (at least in part) what he dreams of doing tomorrow. The distance can be narrowed between his fantasy of "How I *would* fill time" and the reality of "How I *do* fill it." For example:

A sales representative dreamed of working with his hands; so he became a carpenter on weekends.

A truck driver craved intellectual stimulation; he read and wrote books on primate behavior at night.

A psychologist loved seashells; she planned her vacations around their collection.

A housewife returned to college part-time; she later developed into an expert photographer and superb landscape architect.

In short, all of these individuals struggled in their own way with the million-dollar question. In finding partial answers, they brought increased gratification to themselves, and therefore, to their relationships. They began, with no small effort, I think, to put their time and money where their values were.

Achieving Balance

Another path to gratification in leisure activities may be found in the obscure proverb: "A change is as good as a rest." In fact, change may be better than a rest in achieving balanced living.

For instance: To that sales representative, his carpentry involved a change: the "doing" role of craftsman balanced his "talking" role at work. To that truck driver, his books were a change: intellectual efforts balancing physical ones. To the housewife: the stimulation of her camera and garden helped offset the monotony of routine daily work. To the psychologist: the introversion of cataloguing shells at night balanced her extroversion in seeing people all day.

Whereas most of us know the obvious difficulties in breaking old habits, we might start with the recognition that balance is frequently missing in our lives. We should realize that nightly or weekly fatigue may stem not only from overwork (prescription: rest), but also from understimulation, routine, tedium, and boredom (prescription: change).

Time: Alone Versus Together

One of the hardest balances to achieve in marriage is some harmony between time away, time alone, and time together. Being close to a person, yet needing distance from him, was explored in Chapter 1 ("Quiet Time: The Need for Privacy," page 5) and Chapter 3 ("A Time for Distance, a Time for Closeness," page 48). Still, the problem of living together, but seldom being "alone together," requires brief mention here.

At various stages in marriage, we resemble two trains passing in the night; our paths cross only at breakfast, dinner, or bedtime. During the evening, we are often separated by children, meetings, guests, fatigue, T.V. programs . . . an endless list. Over the weekends, beyond Saturday projects and Sunday sports, we are busy in the entertainment of family and friends, acquaintances or associates. Under these circumstances, in the best relationship, we find it difficult to share time alone with each other. We are simply too over-scheduled, over-committed, and over-run by a constant stream of people and activity.

In many homes, of course, such activities become a mutually desirable way of life. They infuse weekly routines with variety and excitement. In other homes, I think, couples run at a frantic pace for different reasons.

The dilemma of saying "no" to people

Although the roots of a pair's not spending time "alone together" are complex, one reason is easy to identify and relatively simple to correct. It occurs when neither husband nor wife can say "no" to other people with diplomacy or comfort. For example, the following dialogue took place in marital therapy and is common to many families.

Husband: One of my wife's biggest hang-ups is saying "no." Someone calls, she accepts or extends an invitation, and then waits days to tell me. When I do learn about it, my first reaction is to blow up and shout: "Dammit, I'm not going!" or, "They're not coming," which I've been saying now for about ten years.

Wife: Which is one reason why it takes me several days to tell him about invitations.

Husband: There's always a scene . . .

Wife: And yet, the problem isn't disagreeing about friends. We agree on ninety percent of them.

Husband: But we end up going places we don't want to go, spending time with people we don't really want to see.

Therapist: Does anything help in saying "no"?

Husband: Yes. Unplugging the telephone.

Wife: Or, a small lie: "My husband may have plans for that night."

Husband: That helps. Still, each phone call is a whole new ball game. She feels ambivalent, agonizes, and more often than not says "yes."

Wife: Him too! God forbid he should answer the phone.

Therapist: Sounds exhausting.

Both: It is.

Therapist: Would you feel guilty about having a standard "out" to all invitations? Such as: "Let me ring back tomorrow—I'll check to see if we have plans for that day."

Wife: Not at all. It would be a great relief to me.

Husband: And me. It would probably take all of ten minutes
            to decide on accepting or rejecting invitations. As
            she said, we do agree on people.

Therapist: But one person must still call back and say "no."

Wife: Better than repeated fights.

Husband: I agree.

Therapist: Why do you suppose it has taken ten years to
            develop such signals?

Husband: Lord knows . . .

Wife: Out of curiosity: How long did it take you and
            your wife to learn about saying "no"?

Therapist: Oh! . . . Ahh . . . About five years.

This ability to defend time serves as valuable and necessary
protection in the preservation of any intimacy between two
people. Learning to say "no" helps us, midst our daily demands
and weekly pressures, to reserve time not only for ourselves, but
for each other.

Time: Quantity Versus Quality

This is not to imply that couples must free-up endless hours to
spend together. As a rule, quality of time is infinitely more important than quantity.

Here, we might draw an analogy to the relationship between
parents and children. When a child pulls at those real or
imaginary apron strings, his demands continue until whatever
ails him is soothed. His needs persist, in spite of his mother's
pleas, shouts, threats, or half-hearted attention. But, when a
parent can make time, especially after work, to spend a concentrated hour with his son or daughter, the child's need for
time together dramatically decreases for that day. In fact, an
hour of undivided attention between parent and child usually
leads to relaxation of tensions as well as the reestablishment of
communication and closeness.

I do not mean to say that if one concentrated hour is good, eight to ten hours are better. In fact, even if a mother is home all day, she cannot spend one hundred percent of her time and energy with children. Nor would such an expenditure be profitable. As children need attention, so too, they need periods of inattention and solitude. Like adults, they want time to be alone. They need privacy.

We might ask at this point: Are intimate relationships between adults so different in this respect from those between parents and children? I don't think so. However, one aspect of the similarity does need further elaboration.

Popular formulas do exist for couples' giving concentrated attention to each other. Such prescriptions often advise husbands and wives to get away together "half a day, each week." Or, "One weekend, every month."* While this advice sounds fine in theory, it seldom works in practice. Why? To return to our analogy: Would these answers help communications between a parent and child? Would one afternoon per week, for example, be sufficient to relax tensions and promote intimacy?

Here, again, I don't think so. Whereas children thrive on daily doses of concentrated attention, so too, I believe, do their parents. In both cases, relationships grow with small amounts of daily loving.

For adults, "quality" time may come in the form of a fifteen-minute review at night or half an hour's conversation over dinner. It may occur during the washing of dishes, playing of dominoes, riding to movies, or gossiping in bed. These brief moments consume only a mere fraction of twenty-four hours; and yet, they are indispensable to the process of two lovers touching base and maintaining closeness. As such, the quality of a couple's time together, measured daily, becomes another cornerstone in the foundation of an intimate relationship.

* Paradoxically, I think couples who do make time for one another "half a day per week" or "one weekend per month" are frequently men and women in good communication with each other. Talking on a daily basis, they are less frightened at the prospect of spending time alone together.

7

Practice: Married or Not

> Practice implies repeated performances for the purpose of learn-
> ing or acquiring proficiency (. . . *practice* makes perfect).
> —WEBSTER'S DICTIONARY

Why are so many couples reluctant to practice with each other
and with their sexual relationship? "The difficulty is . . ." explain two people at the end of an exhausting day, "we're too
tired." Or, husbands and wives ask with genuine bewilder-
ment: "What do you mean by practicing at home?"

How strange it is that practice, normal for children and
natural for adults, seems so abnormal and unnatural for married
couples. What follows in this chapter, therefore, are brief discussions of: (1) child's practice, (2) adult's practice, (3) marital
practice, (4) barriers to practice—and in a shift to a more popularized problem, (5) premarital sex as practice, and in more
detail, (6) premarital living as practice.

Practice in Childhood

In most societies, practice consumes the lion's share of a child's
day. At home or school, learning is the "work" of young people.
An infant spends hour upon hour learning to grasp, roll over,

sit, crawl, and walk. A boy or girl commits several hours every day in school learning how to read and write, divide and multiply, speak English or French, and so forth. At recess as well, "child's play" is synonymous with "child's practice." On playgrounds, boys and girls learn to kick footballs or serve volleyballs. And, in the process, they master not only how to punt or volley balls, but how to share with teammates and classmates. On the playing fields as well as off them.

After school, practice doesn't cease for most youngsters. Indeed, from music lessons to homework, parents teach that mastery over one's flute or fractions comes from daily practice (as does mastery over one's feelings).

In addition, when a child does make mistakes in the pursuit of new goals, reasonable parents allow their sons and daughters a wide margin of error. Falling on his face is not only permissible, but predictable in a child's day. The toddler falls. The two-year-old mispronounces new words. The ten-year-old misspells hard ones. In most homes, parents show a high tolerance for these "mistakes." They know that trial and error is a vital part of growth and development—be that development called walking, talking, spelling, or expressing emotions. As such, practice becomes a way of life for most children.

Practice in Adulthood

What about adult practice? Does not "practice makes perfect" have obvious and widespread application to grown-ups? Of course. Outside the home, for instance, most adult success is based upon the principle of daily practice. Surgeons spend every day for a decade learning their art before making a living at it. Zen Buddhists practice at meditation one to three hours every morning for a lifetime. Actors and musicians rehearse eight to ten hours a day for a performance. As do athletes who train for Olympic or professional competition. From gourmet chefs to master carpenters, writers to farmers, scientists to businessmen, long hours over many years seem clearly necessary to achieve excellence in one's work. In one's home, however, we might ask: How many hours do most couples devote to the achievement of excellence in their private relationship?

Marital Practice

For most of us, "Practice: Married or Not" implies men and women having numerous premarital affaires. Or married couples buying the latest sex book and following directions. By "practice," however, I do not mean only the improvement of sexual technique; nor do I mean practice as limited to New Year's resolutions, such as: "I'll be more patient with the children," or "less angry with my wife" (this year). What I mean by practice is more a daily effort than an annual event. It is more "general" than "sexual."

For example: Let us review the need for practice as illustrated by the way couples learn to ask for privacy in marriage: It often takes two people several years to appreciate that conflicting desires to love and to leave the other person are not incompatible. In many families, husbands and wives often spend those years translating an inner reaction—"I need to get away from you"—into an excuse to leave home. As I previously mentioned: forgotten errands or frequent emergencies, week-night appointments or weekend arrangements, all become escape routes to the outside world.

Most couples require years to realize that "I must get out of here" need not always be the other person's fault. Indeed, that peace and quiet are necessities in all good sexual relationships. Yet, it does take practice to recognize the feelings "I don't want to talk" or "I can't listen" as helpful warning signs. Additionally, couples need to practice turning such signals into positive requests: "I'd like some quiet time" . . . "Where's my newspaper or knitting?" . . . "I want to unwind." Requests which say, in effect: "It's not that I need to get away from *you*." But rather, "*I* need to fill up." (Although these phrases may seem simple enough in books, they realistically require months to years of constant practice before an individual feels comfortable saying them.)

Thus, practicing with each other, couples can learn not only that the stimulus for privacy flows from an inner need. But also, quiet time within marriage can be requested without leaving home or without hurting the other person.

Or, let us take practice in the expression of compliments, sexual and nonsexual. In bed, many people find it hard to say anything. It is difficult for them to voice their feelings, even positive ones, during intercourse. Such lovers may think: "It's good to feel so close" . . . "I love you" . . . "I need you." . . . But instead of speaking, they remain silent. How can such a person begin to practice the sharing of his pleasurable feelings during lovemaking?

Paradoxically, many men and women begin when not making love. They find it easier to practice expressions of affection outside the bedroom. It's less embarrassing for them to offer praise during nonsexual hours. They may also discover not only that compliments are more easily practiced during the daylight rather than nighttime, but also, they are easier to practice with one's children than with one's spouse.

Few mothers and fathers, for example, would consider praise of their children as "practice." They would not be reluctant to say "I love you" or "my wonderful son" or "my fantastic daughter." Nor would most parents feel awkward acknowledging a job well done by their children with such expressions as "Terrific!" . . . "Unbelievable!" . . . "Super!" . . . "Perfect!" Consequently, for an inhibited person in bed, praise of little ones may offer an initial springboard to praise of a partner.

The next step, of course, is to practice the display of affection directly with one's husband or wife. And again, such practice may be easier during the day. I have previously emphasized the vital role of daily praise in good relationships. (See Chapter 2: "Praise: The Minimum Daily Requirement.") To review briefly: It proves extremely helpful when two people voice their support and compliments of each other in everyday situations, such as a man's saying when: (1) calling his wife: "I just wanted to touch base." . . . "I miss you." (2) coming home: "The house looks nice." . . . "You look nice." . . . "It's good to be home." (3) eating meals: "What a dinner, you've done it again." . . . "I've rattled on about my day, how was yours?" Or either partner's saying "Thank you" for anything from doing dishes to seeing movies: "I'm glad you thought of it." . . . "That's exactly what I needed tonight." . . . "Thanks love."

My point about couples' verbalizing their positive feelings may seem repetitious. But, I think, there exists a direct relationship between how easily two people can say "I love you" or "wonderful" or "That's just what I needed"—before and after lights-out. In other words: Should two lovers practice and learn to express praise (when they feel it) out of bed, praise in bed becomes that much easier.

To develop new habits or behavior in marriage, there is simply no substitute for practicing that behavior. Be it called: "Daily Praise," "A Fifteen Minute Review at Night," "A House Rule: We Never Go to Bed Mad," "Asking for Privacy," "Signaling Sexual Needs—This Month, This Week. . . ." In all cases, it goes without saying that practice does help make perfect.

Barriers to Practice: Doing What Comes (Un)Naturally

Many barriers to practice go back to a person's childhood. As men and women have frequently asked in my office: "How can I practice expressing anger? Growing up, I was taught that nice little girls (boys) don't get mad." Others have said: "Display affection outside the bedroom? It's darn hard after thirty years of not displaying it. As a child I never did see my mother kiss my father in front of us kids." While others have asked: "Be supportive? Would you believe I can't remember my parents ever saying to me: 'You did a good job.' Let alone: 'I love you.' "

Yet, not all barriers are so deeply stated in one's past history. Many of us don't practice within our relationship simply because we won't commit the necessary time, effort, and energy to the private side of our lives. Working hard all day, we have neither the hours nor the interest to do more "work" at night. We're too tired. And consequently, exhaustion from twenty-five-hour days, on the job or with the children, becomes a natural stumbling block to nightly practice.

Aside from fatigue, however, there's another equally common cause for the failure of two people to practice at home. It is one person's *basic fear of looking ridiculous* to the other person, whenever he or she attempts something new. The following concerns were voiced during an early session in marital therapy and illustrate the point.

Wife: I can't show anger.

Therapist: Can you show affection?

Wife: I have trouble.

Therapist: When your husband comes home from work, do you ever give him a little peck, squeeze, or hug before dinner?

Wife: *Very* seldom. He's better at expressing feelings than I am.

Therapist: Why is it so hard for you?

Wife: I really don't know.

Husband: (Kidding on the square.) She's probably afraid I'd be so surprised and delighted that I might rape her.

Therapist: (To the wife.) Is that what you're afraid of—being raped?

Wife: As a matter of fact, in our first year of marriage, whenever I kissed him during the day, he'd go crazy. Like an adolescent high school boy on his first date. Any show of affection on my part always led to our making love.

Therapist: Is that still true?

Wife: Not really. Maybe the problem now is that I'm afraid of looking dumb. And feeling dumb. After twelve years of marriage, how do you suddenly start hugging or kissing your husband for no apparent reason without feeling a bit ridiculous?

In this case, the husband could help his wife by being sensitive to her vulnerability. When she attempts to act differently in their relationship, he needs to recognize her feeling "dumb" as a potential barrier to new behavior. Thus, should his wife hug or squeeze him after work, it would not be helpful for him to confirm her worst fears with such remarks as: "What are you doing?" and "Don't be ridiculous!" Nor would it be helpful for the husband to say nothing and pull away from his wife. Clearly, such verbal and nonverbal messages would only serve to undermine rather than support her efforts to make changes.

The situation is not unlike that wife who finally mustered the courage to practice in bed after seven years of marriage. The woman who ultimately mentioned "breasts" to her husband as she explained the meaning of "Kiss me, kiss me" after intercourse. In that case, the wife also felt silly experimenting with new behavior after many years of marriage. And she, too, would have felt shattered if her husband had responded: "Kiss your breasts *after* lovemaking? Are you kidding?" . . . "Have you been reading one of those sex books?" . . . "But, good grief, I want to sleep after making love."

Such comments as "What are you doing?" and "Don't be ridiculous!" would only reinforce any wife's feelings of inadequacy. They would insure that, having exposed herself and having been hurt by it, she'd be extremely reluctant to practice in other ways and at other times.

Practice usually involves the husband or wife feeling insecure and taking chances. Practice of something new means one person's exposure to potential hurt by another person. As such, it is the opposite of a couple's "playing-it-safe." Practice is a risk under the best circumstances; but it is impossible when two partners don't respect each other's feeling "exposed" or "vulnerable," "ridiculous" or "dumb" when they're attempting to break new ground with the person they love.

Premarital Sex As Practice

Let us now shift focus and turn to a more traditional view of practice. Let us ask: What about sexual experience before marriage?

In 1953, Dr. Alfred Kinsey reported that of women born between 1920 and 1929, four percent had premarital intercourse by age fifteen and twenty-one percent by age twenty.* In a recent study of unmarried teenage women,† the incidence was shown to be: fourteen percent by age fifteen; forty-six percent by age nineteen. (Note: The proportion of teenagers now having premarital coitus is actually higher, as about sixty percent of married teenagers report having had intercourse before marriage.)

* Alfred Kinsey, *Sexual Behavior in the Human Female* (Philadelphia, W. B. Saunders Company, 1953) page 339.

† For a summary report on one part of a 1971 survey of 4,240 never-married fifteen- to nineteen-year-olds, see J. F. Kantner and M. Zelnik, "Sexual Experiences of Young Unmarried Women in the United States," *Family Planning Perspectives*, Vol. 4, No. 4 (October, 1972) page 9. The report is taken from the author's larger study published in C. F. Westoff and R. Parke, Jr., eds., *Demographic and Social Aspects of Population Growth* (Washington, D.C., U.S. Government Printing Office, 1972) pages 355 to 374.

Past teenage, Dr. Kinsey reported that one-third of single women had had intercourse by age twenty-five. Whereas another recent survey* noted this figure had more than doubled, and about three-quarters of single women now admit to having premarital relations by twenty-five.

As for single males, they are beginning intercourse earlier in life. For example, Kinsey reported two-thirds of noncollege males had had premarital sex by age seventeen. The Playboy statistics show that figure to be nearly three-quarters by the same age. For men with some college education, over half have now had premarital coitus at seventeen. For Kinsey's group, only a quarter were that sexually active.

How do these findings compare with worldwide attitudes on the subject? A Gallup International Poll in mid-1973 asked the eighteen- to twenty-four-year-olds of ten nations if they agreed with the following statement: Premarital sexual relations *should be avoided under any circumstances.*† Those in agreement from each nation:

Sweden	4%
West Germany	6%
Switzerland	8%
France	10%
United Kingdom	14%
Yugoslavia	18%
United States	23%
Japan	27%
Brazil	40%
India	73%

All of these statistics would indicate that more young people today approve of and engage in premarital sex than did thirty

* The Playboy Foundation through the Research Guild, Inc., of Chicago surveyed 2,026 people in twenty-four urban areas. Results of their findings began being published in *Playboy* (October, 1973) pages 85ff. A book-length treatment of the survey, *Sexual Behavior in the 1970's* by Morton Hunt, is scheduled for publication in Spring 1974.

† The American Institute of Public Opinion (The Gallup Poll).

years ago. Yet, in spite of this "revolution" or "renaissance," support for intercourse before marriage remains far from unanimous.

Northern California's largest morning newspaper, for example, during the fall of 1972 asked seven adults in random man-on-the-street interviews: "Is Premarital Sex Good for a Happy Marriage?"* The respondents included:

An organic metals representative (male) who said: "I'm not for it. It destroys the moral fiber in each person if they commit this act . . . "

An insurance typist (female): "I don't condemn it, but it's up to the people involved whether it would be good or bad . . . "

An employment case worker (male): "Well, it usually makes it easier to choose a good sex partner and then a good marriage partner . . . "

An insurance underwriter (male): "I can't believe so, but I'm from the old-fashioned school. They should both come into the marriage virgins . . . "

A shipping messenger (male): "Yes, because you get to know the person totally before. There's so many moral things, so many hangups a person can have, that you might be wise to have long courtships that include sex . . . "

A steamship receptionist (female): "Yes. Definitely. You get to know each other better and find out what it's all about. You have to have knowledge of sex and it's better to come into marriage with that knowledge . . . "

A railroad engineer (male): "That depends on the individuals. The man should have some sex before. . . . Most men would feel pretty foolish going into a marriage as a virgin. Women shouldn't do it though . . . "

Obviously, the "pro" and "con" of premarital sex remains a highly charged topic. An individual's decision to have or not to have intercourse before matrimony remains an extremely personal matter. One's choices clearly depend upon a host of com-

* *San Francisco Chronicle,* September 30, 1972.

plicated considerations which have been well described in a previous reference.* Here, let us sidestep this issue of premarital sex and turn to a broader question. A question more relevant to the book's theme of the "other 23 hours and 59 minutes" in a couple's life together.

Premarital Living As Practice

For an increasing population of adolescents and adults, the growing question is not only: "Is premarital sex good for a happy marriage?" but "How valuable is premarital living?" Or, more specifically: "Should we live together if we love each other?"

To answer this dilemma, I have tried to present an abbreviated list of arguments "for" and "against" two people living with one another before marriage—a check list for couples who are debating this problem, alone or with their loved-one. Let us begin with the negative considerations:

Arguments against

1. Young or inexperienced couples may feel a sense of "no exit" when living together twenty-four hours a day, seven days a week. Under one roof, two people cannot escape to their separate worlds after eight or forty-eight hours in each other's presence. There is no such thing as a conventional "date" ending at midnight or 2:00 A.M. Nor an unconventional weekend which ends on Sunday evening or Monday morning. At no time can such couples return to their own home or apartment, lock the door, breathe a sigh of relief, and relax: "I'm alone again. (Thank God!)"

Limits to intimacy (be they called Sunday nights or separate apartments), like those edges to pools, offer most of us an appropriate time and place to catch our breath. In sex or swimming we

---

* See Wardell B. Pomeroy, *Boys and Sex* and *Girls and Sex* referred to on page 72.

tend to learn better not only in a step-by-step fashion, but also, with periodic returns to places of safety.

Thus, should a couple's premarital living not provide an "edge-of-the-pool" effect, constant togetherness may prove an unnecessarily frightening (indeed, "wrong") way to learn about lasting sexual relationships. The sink-or-swim approach may simply cause two new lovers to drown in too much intimacy, too soon.

2. Again, for young and inexperienced couples: Living together can narrow rather than expand horizons. One result of early commitment, married or not, is the ruling out of learning with multiple partners. Not only can it limit sexual learning, but it can also put a lid on learning about other important life experiences, such as: same-sex friendships, opposite-sex friendships, commitment to ideals or causes, further schooling, or extensive traveling.

For example: High school sweethearts who meet at fifteen, go steady at sixteen, live together at eighteen, and marry at twenty often have predictable problems in their future relationship. Part of the trouble stems from the fact that such couples do not know what an intimate relationship, good or bad, is like with various partners. They only know about two other people's private lives from gossip columns, advice columns, magazines, films, novels, and their limited exposure to other people. It's seldom enough. Consequently, fantasies run wild. With little or no previous sexual and nonsexual contact, these two lovers can't help but think, "What did I miss?" or "With more experience, I'd know what I want." Or, at least "I'd better appreciate what I have."

3. Should premarital living cause excessive guilt feelings, it is not a good test of how two lovers might interact with each other in a future marriage. Broadly speaking, there are two sources for these feelings: One's guilt factory may be stoked from within, due to conflicts of conscience, morality, values, or religious teaching. Or, it may stem from outside pressures such

as family, friends, neighbors, or community. For instance, I know a twenty-five-year-old devout Catholic girl who tried living with her prospective husband before marriage. After two weeks, however, she gave up because "It was so painful that our relationship became unreal. My feeling guilty all the time consumed most of our energy."

I also know a Jewish widow and widower in their early seventies who lived in the southwestern United States. Surprisingly, they were urged by a rabbi to live together before formalizing their planned marriage. More surprisingly, they agreed with him. But, "How could we do it in a small town of five thousand people?" they asked in a realistic question.

To live with strong guilt feelings, regardless of the source, is the wrong climate in which to begin a good sexual relationship.

4. Like premarital pregnancy, premarital living often creates increased pressure for an early marriage. Again, couples must resist the voices from within: "After all these months (years), how can I say 'no'?" As well as the chorus from outside advisors, be they friends or family, "What will people say?" "It's the 'right' thing to do." Or, more guilt-producing statements like, "You mean all of these years (months) were for nothing?"

As with pregnancy as a pressure to marry, I believe that such reasons are unfortunate ones upon which to build a lasting marriage.

5. Another reason against living together, especially at an early age: Dissolution of an intimate relationship tends to undermine one (if not both) partner's self-confidence and self-esteem. Married or not, rejection by someone we love cannot be rationalized: "It didn't work out because he never knew 'the real me.'" On the contrary. Living together implies opening ourselves as totally as possible to another person. Maybe he doesn't know us. But, if he doesn't—who does?

Consequently, our being rejected understandably leads to feelings of anger, worthlessness, frustration, and loneliness. Such reactions, in turn, often cause us to be more defensive with the next person, the next time around. No one wants to be burned twice. Let alone four, five, or six times. And so, at this point we must ask: How many "burnings" before a man feels insecure and hopeless about his capacity to love and to be loved? How many "dissolutions," officially or unofficially, before a woman grows cynical not only about men, but about her own ability to sustain a long-term relationship?

6. Similar questions form the basis of another risk in pre-marital living. How many "failures" are helpful in preparation for marriage? Is the number different for men and women? How many times, for example, can a woman live with a man before she crosses the line from being-in-love to being exploited to being promiscuous? How many women-in-residence can the man keep before he no longer means what he says—because he has said it all too many times before? How much experience does the bride look for in her future husband? And vice versa? Can a person be "too experienced" as well as too inexperienced? How much past history is enough to turn off the other person?

Personally, I believe it is much easier to raise such questions than to answer them. Ultimately, of course, individual answers will hinge upon a person's maturity, sexual experience, parental teaching, religious background, and peer pressures. Global an-swers seldom help with these dilemmas. But, denial of such dilemmas doesn't help either.

7. Finally, with some couples, an argument can be made that their premarital living is more a convenience than a commit-ment. Sexual convenience ("Making love is no longer a prob-lem.") or financial convenience ("Two can live as cheaply as one.") are the main reasons for their living under one roof. Yet, lasting sexual relations demand that two people do eventually commit themselves to each other. Uncommitted, a man and woman may find it too easy to walk away from one another. They can make excuses for not putting in the time, energy, and sacrifices necessary to make any relationship not only work, but last. As such, I think an absence of mutual commitment and

shared responsibility bodes poorly for the long-range success of a couple's living together.

Arguments for

Let us now turn to the positive reasons for men and women sharing a nonmarital arrangement. By "arrangement," however, I am not proposing yet another new life-style. In fact, I have in mind couples living together under guidelines previously suggested by Judge Ben B. Lindsey of Colorado.* As a juvenile court magistrate in Denver, he proposed many years ago that young people be allowed to enter into a "companionate marriage." An institution which differed from regular marriage in three basic ways:

1. Initially, a couple should have no intention of having children. Thus, contraceptive information should be freely available and routinely used by two partners enjoying this kind of relationship.
2. Divorce would be possible by mutual consent as long as the wife wasn't pregnant and there were no children.
3. There should be no alimony if the marriage were to end in divorce.

A radical suggestion in answer to today's youth? Not really. Judge Lindsey's trial marriage was outlined by him in 1927.

Now, almost fifty years later, the positive reasons for such arrangements might differ somewhat from the Judge's original arguments. At either time, however, a case could be made that trial marriages† help two embryonic lovers to lower defenses and remove masks. With the result: A pair's illusions and realities about one another might start to merge before the wedding ceremony rather than after it.

* Judge Ben B. Lindsey and Wainwright Evans, *The Companionate Marriage* (New York, Boni & Liveright, 1927).

† From Leon Blum in France to Margaret Mead in America, the concept of trial marriage is a familiar one in the twentieth century.

Why?

Because living-together couples can't hold their breath or put their best face forward until a date ends at 2:00 A.M., a weekend with each other stops on Sunday night, or a vacation together runs its course in seven to twenty-one days. In this sense, there's no "edge-of-the-pool" effect for two lovers sharing one house. And, as such, living together before marriage may be a more realistic way for couples to learn about themselves and one another. More realistic, at least, for those lovers who plan to sink-or-swim together for the rest of their life.

Another positive reason for the companionate-style marriage was offered by Bertrand Russell. Defending the concept of premarital living arrangements, Lord Russell said in the late 1920's: "It seems absurd to ask people to enter upon a relation intended to be lifelong without any previous knowledge as to their sexual compatibility."*

In the mid 1970s, paradoxically, I would add that it seems equally foolish to ask couples to enter upon the difficult business of marriage (a "trial" in itself) without also testing their non-sexual compatibilities.

Assuming that two people can live together relatively free of painful guilt or punitive sanctions, they have an opportunity before "till death do us part" to practice the essentials of married life. Practice supporting each other, conversing together, developing signals, resolving arguments. They have a chance to see how their chosen partner spends not only his time, but his money. On a day-to-day, week-to-week, month-to-month basis. They have an opportunity to learn how flexible is their future husband or wife, in making changes as well as making love. In short, under the same roof, two lovers can better test their sexual and nonsexual compatibilities (a) before deciding to have children, and (b) before tying a legal and religious knot, with all of its binding implications.

* Bertrand Russell, *Marriage and Morals* (New York, Bantam Books, 1959) (Liveright, 1929), pages 112–113.

8

Sexual Roles: Beyond
"Me, Tarzan. You, Jane."

The question of proper roles for men and women has been widely debated over the past decade. This chapter's purpose, however, is not to enter into that debate. Consequently, for a man who wants to hear: "The husband should wear the pants." or, for a woman hoping to read: "The wife should (shouldn't) be liberated" or, for the couple who seek a more poetic metaphor, such as: "The man is a ship. His wife a harbor," the following chapter may prove a disappointment.

With the ongoing confusion, controversy, and anger over male and female functions, it is more important than ever that couples help each other define their own roles within a specific relationship. Avoiding the eye of the current hurricane, I have purposely side-stepped the general question: What are appropriate masculine and feminine functions in marriage?* Instead, I have tried to answer in this chapter: (a) How can one lover's

* For an eloquent perspective and description of familial roles, I highly recommend *Family* by Margaret Mead and Ken Heyman (New York, Collier Books, 1971). In thoughtful prose and photographs, the authors examine the world of mothers, fathers, sisters, brothers, grandparents, friends, adolescents, the child alone, and the family itself.

Also, for an exceptional and scholarly work on the psychological role of women in history, myth, and today's world, see Wolfgang Lederer, M.D., *The Fear of Women* (New York, Harcourt Brace Jovanovich, 1968).

role expectations for the other be discussed in everyday situations and everyday language? and (b) How can such discussions help two people become more flexible and less frozen in relating to one another?

Clarification of Roles

When problems are small

In some homes, roles in daily living are handled by the house rule: "See what needs to be done—and do it." Thus, who washes dishes or takes out garbage depends upon which person has more free time on that particular night. Neutral duties such as who feeds the dog, covers the kids, starts the bath water, locks up the house, turns out lights, never reach the point of being assigned and defined on a regular basis. Because husband and wife expect each other spontaneously to pitch in with routine chores, they never do clarify responsibility for the performance of trivial tasks. At least for these couples "pitching-in" on daily chores proves to be an ideal arrangement.

For most couples, however, lack of role clarification may prove unbelievably time consuming. (See "Making Decisions," page 38.) It may lead two people to sit around the living room night after night wondering, silently or aloud, after dinner: "Who's going to do dishes tonight?" Or, before bed: "Did you empty the trash?" . . . "close the garage?" . . . "check the children?" . . . "turn off the stove?" . . . "lock the door?"

Not only can this Alfonse and Gaston routine ("Should I? . . . Should I?") drain one's energies, but it can also produce hostile feelings. After several years of one partner's *not* seeing obvious needs and filling them, his husband or wife can understandably become annoyed and impatient. Such feelings, in turn, can lead to anger over nightly roles, arguments about dishes or garbage, and tension created by the "I always . . . you never," kind of resentments which tend to develop in these situations. Thus, a couple's preoccupations with simple daily duties can prove exhausting.

As I mentioned in Chapter 3: "When questions over nightly chores become sources of friction, it often helps to ask (and answer): 'Who does what?' or 'Who is responsible?' " Here, a familiar vignette illustrates the energy wasted when two people don't clarify their minor responsibilities at night.

A husband and wife, married almost two years, would entertain friends at home several times per month. Although they liked the concept of being gracious with guests, they kept stumbling over each other in their roles as host and hostess. Their last minute preparations for dinner parties always included variations on the following dialogue:

Husband: There's the door bell. Honey . . . would you answer it. I'm busy checking the liquor supply . . .

Wife: Can't, Love. I'm in the middle of hors d'oeuvres.

Husband: Okay, I'll answer it. But remember, I need you to entertain everyone for about ten minutes while I fix drinks. No hiding in the kitchen tonight.

Wife: But, Darling . . . if I talk, dinner will burn.

Husband: (*Turning*) Forget it. I'll get the door and get the drinks. They can talk without us for a few minutes.

Wife: (*Stopping him*) Luv, after drinks, will you seat people for dinner?

Husband: Dammit. You know I always screw up and put the wrong people next to each other. Quick, tell me, where should Bill and Nancy go?

Wife: Oh . . . I don't know. What do you think?

Husband: I think that I'd better answer the door.

Caricature and Emily Post aside, I don't believe that it really matters whether husband *or* wife seats Bill and Nancy, Bob and

Carol, and so forth. Nor does it matter who answers doorbells, takes coats, pours drinks, serves hors d'oeuvres, cooks dinner, or makes conversation. Like emptying garbage or feeding pets, it only matters that such mini-roles get clarified, so that this unnecessary and repetitious duplication of effort and waste of two people's energy comes to an end.

When problems are large

Should clarity help husband and wife in minor crises, it can also help them during major conflicts. For example, it may help couples in their more significant role expectations for the other person. Another familiar situation demonstrates the point.

In many families, a wife plays the role of mother and father to her children throughout most of the week. Since her husband is more absent than present during the children's waking hours, Mom's substituting for Dad Monday through Friday isn't that unusual. Nor is it unusual, when Saturday comes, that problems ensue over "Who does what?" with the kids. Frequently, the root of the problem lies in a couple's conflicting expectations for the other person.

Many working fathers have definite ideas about their spouse's role during weekends. Because the man wants to relax and unwind, he expects his wife's help on Saturdays and Sundays. For one thing: Weekends are his only mornings to sleep-in. Consequently, Dad may want Mom to hold down not only the fort, but also, the children's noise levels for an extra one or two hours. (At all cost . . . to her.) In addition, he may expect equal protection while he putters in the garden or works in the basement. As well as protection during those football games which consume his Saturday or Sunday afternoons.

Regardless of where he elects to hide on weekends, however, such a father's message is clear. He is saying in effect: "Everyone just leave me alone." So, when interrupted by the inevitable

demands of wife and children, it is not surprising that many husbands become righteously indignant and think:

"I can't even have some peace and quiet in my own house."
"I should really leave home for a few days."
"No one appreciates me. Who the hell do you think pays the bills
around here?!"
"I'm going crazy . . . "
"Just leave me alone."

Meanwhile, of course, the wife lies in bed on weekend mornings caught between two realities: Her children's demands and
her husband's erection. To whom does she owe her allegiance?
What is her role? What does she want? She also has her own
expectations for being left alone on weekends. Expectations
which frequently run 180 degrees opposite to those of her husband. Playing dual roles from Monday through Friday, the wife
understandably expects some relief from children on Saturday
and Sunday. As she waits for her husband to provide that relief,
feelings of "I always . . . you never . . . " simmer within her.
Angry and martyred by his delaying tactics, she may boil over
with such feelings as:

"I always do everything . . . you never do anything."
"If you don't want to spend time with us—the hell with you."
"You don't care about us."
"I can't stand it anymore. Not a minute to myself. I can't even go
to the bathroom."
"There's no escape . . . "
"I'm going crazy . . . "

If such are the reactions, at least in part, of husbands and
wives over parental roles on weekends—wherein lies the answer
for these "irreconcilable differences?" One solution, I think, begins with a couple's discussing the problem and clarifying their
functions. In discussing weekend expectations, for instance, it is
legitimate and helpful that a husband clarify his desire for periods of quiet time away from the kids. It is also appropriate that
a wife define the children's need for their father. As well as her

own need to let down on Saturday and Sunday. This admission of differences helps two people begin to understand each other's hopes and expectations. It also helps them to reach compromises. For example, the wife might suggest:

"Look. You expect me to quiet the kids and I expect you to disappear with them. We usually spend weekends angry at one another for not being sensitive to each other's needs. Lately, I get furious when you sleep till nine, escape to the basement, or watch television during the only two days you're home. But I wouldn't get so furious (I think) if I could also disappear for a few hours."

"Maybe it would help to set up definite times for you to have the children. What if both of us expected you to take the kids, say, from eight to eleven in the mornings, or three to six every afternoon on Saturday and Sunday? At least we'd be on the same wavelength about our expectations for some privacy. Hopefully, we might relax and not be so irritable with one another. What do you think about the idea?"

I realize that many people would find this couple's answer too simplistic or too rigid; inappropriate for their own style of handling problems around weekend roles. Yet, other couples might like the notion of a relatively straightforward solution to an obviously complicated problem. Or, they would like to know more about the means (that is, discussion and clarification) to achieve their own ends.

However, they might also realistically say, "We do talk, but nothing ever happens." And in the next four sections I have attempted to deal with this problem in more detail.

Talking and Doing: The Key to Changing Roles

The "talking" part

We can start with the fact that changes in roles are made easier when husband and wife teach one another about their role expectations. Like asking for support ("When Problems are Obvious," page 25), our requests are more likely to become realities if we can simplify matters by: (1) identifying the problem, and (2) suggesting an answer. From entertaining one's guests to entertaining one's children, it helps to say what we need under the circumstances. For example: In a minor change over that hostess' role:

Identified Problem: "I can't be with our guests and fix drinks
(*by the husband*) at the same time."
Suggested Solution: "Could you entertain them for ten minutes while I'm filling orders?"

Or, in a major change over the father's role:

Identified Problem: "We both wait all day for each other to
(*by the wife*) take the kids on Saturday and Sunday."
Suggested Solution: "If you took the children over the weekend at definite times, we'd both know what to expect."

Before proceeding, however, let us ask: How helpful are such two-line examples?

I believe they are helpful only as abbreviated shorthand for a complicated process. They, like any cookbook kind of recipe, are much easier to read than to put into practice. Indeed, mastery over new roles takes not days or weeks, but years.

As yet a final example, the next dialogue fills only half a page in this book. (It lasted about one minute in my office.) But, in reality, it summarized almost one year of a couple's persistent efforts to change the husband's role, during periods of his wife's hurting at home.

Wife: Throughout our six-year marriage, I always felt that he never wanted to hear my problems. I knew that he didn't like my getting angry . . . or nervous

. . . or tearful in the evening. So, I just began to put the lid on all of my feelings.

Husband: She's right. At the end of my day, I didn't want to hear any more problems. (In fact, I still don't.)

Wife: Subsequently, whenever I felt mad . . . or sad . . . I'd end up going to our bedroom and crying alone.

Husband: In turn, I'd get damn annoyed at her. I'd just know: "Here we go again."

Wife: With the result: I'd withdraw. He'd withdraw. And it might be a week before we'd close the distance between us.

Husband: We argued for months without any resolution of the problem.

Wife: It took about six months for me to tell him what I needed on those nights.

Husband: And another six months for me to do it. Now, though, if I can honestly give her what she obviously needs—me and sympathy—we can usually resolve things before bed.

The "doing part" or the giving of "me and sympathy"

Here, too, changes in the husband's role can be abbreviated in the same shorthand. His wife:

Identified the problem:	(*Saying in effect*) "Do you realize that I never discuss my problems or my feelings with you?"
	and
Suggested an answer:	All I really need when I'm hurting at night is an hour of your attention and your support.

In proposing these changes, however, the wife does not operate in a vacuum. To achieve results, the couple has to go beyond the "talking" stage of discussing problems and offering suggestions to the "doing" phase of action upon those suggestions. Such actions may begin with one partner's hurt, yet they ultimately depend upon the other partner's help. In other words: If there is to be successful teaching, there must also be successful learning. Thus, hard as it may have been in this case for the wife to start: "It took half a year to admit the problem and tell him what I needed." Final success rested with the husband's action: "It took another six months for me to put her suggestion into practice."

Here, the key to role change is not unlike the key to any change. Regarding the identification of problems as a first step to change—be it over sex, roles, or whatever—I have previously alluded to a fundamental reality: Asking for change, two people must love and trust each other. Trust, because the person asking for some form of new behavior must know that his request will not produce personal attacks from the person he loves. He must believe that the wife's or husband's initial hurt will lead to understanding; anger to action; his need for defensiveness to a need for pleasing the other person. *Ultimately, it is the desire of two people to please one another that creates the supportive atmosphere so necessary for the development of new habits.* A climate in which couples can define problems (in this case over roles), request changes, offer suggestions, and act upon those suggestions.

Beyond the Anger I

Why do so many couples report: "We do talk—but life seldom changes?" One reason is, in a word, anger. Anger is an unfortunate, but predictable, hurdle that often lies between talking and doing something about roles. As one wife put her dilemma: "Should I discuss changes with my husband, it always results in an argument." Because "talking about roles means fighting over them" she concluded, "why talk?"

For various reasons, many of us cannot discuss a shift in roles without a fight over them. We never go from words to deeds because we keep getting hung up in the intervening fights. No sooner have we begun to discuss changes in roles, large or small, when we find ourselves engaged in an infantile struggle over them. For example, that battle over role of host and hostess might have produced the following exchange:

He: Why can't you talk with people for ten minutes while I fix drinks?

She: I can.

He: Then why don't you?

She: Because, whenever I talk in public, you criticize me for saying too much . . . or saying the wrong thing.

He: No, I don't.

She: Yes, you do.

He: Oh no, I don't . . .

She: Oh yes, you do . . .

Or, anger in that discussion about parental roles over weekends. It might have included these familiar barbs and digs:

Wife: I can never have any privacy on Saturday and Sunday.

Husband: You can't! What about me?

Wife: You?

Husband: Yes, me.

Wife: Are you kidding? You disappear all weekend.

Husband: Me, disappear?

Wife: You watch T.V. all day Sunday, don't you?

Husband: You call three hours of football all day?

Wife: I wish I had three hours.

Husband: You could have it.

Wife: When?

Husband: Whenever you like . . .

Wife: Talk's cheap . . .

Or, for the last couple who said: "We argued for months without any resolution of the problem." Their arguments probably produced words to the effect:

She: You never listen to my problems.

He: What do you mean? I listen to your problems every night.

She: You don't.

He: I do.

She: When was the last time you heard me say, "I'm hurting . . . "

He: I always . . .

She: You never . . .

In most cases, I think that it proves helpful if we expect such run-of-the-mill hostilities in the initial discussion over roles. Predictable hostilities over being a better host or hostess, father or mother, talker or listener. Predictable anger, especially if we don't talk on a regular basis, manifested by the "I always . . . you never" and "Yes, I do . . . no, you don't" choruses so familiar to most of us. Familiar refrains which explode after weeks or months of our putting the lid on simmering resentments.

My point is that a couple's task is to get beyond these resentments. To view "I always . . . you never" as an initial phase. To see "Yes, I do . . . no, you don't . . . Goddamnit, YES I DO!" as an inevitable barrier which must be overcome before rational discussions of role differences can occur between two people. To know that reasonable solutions can't be found at unreasonable moments. And, in this perspective, to realize that anger can become the first instead of the last stop on the way to clarification of family functions.

Of course, some husbands and wives move from discussion of roles to arguments over them and they reach an impasse at that point. Their ability to predict anger doesn't realistically help them to go beyond it. Thus, we might ask: What else helps couples as they reach such an impasse?

Beyond the Anger II:
Seeing the Forest Instead of the Twigs

Like arguments over orgasm, some arguments over roles block a couple's view of their other twenty-four hours. In the case of roles: Should two people be constantly battling over functions which require only several minutes in their day (such as who makes the bed, picks up clothes, shops for groceries, or drives the children), it may be helpful to look beyond the twigs—of sheets or shopping, picking up clothes or picking up children—to the forest of daily living. Especially when a wife's anger seems out of all proportion to her husband's crime (or vice versa), it may be time for such couples to look for problems elsewhere in their relationship.

Not wanting to sound too much like the caricature of a psychiatrist, I hasten to add that in many families "I wish you'd not leave your dirty socks on the floor" means only "I wish you'd not leave your dirty socks on the floor." In other families, however, I know of situations where "You never help me" means that "You're never home to help me." Where "I do all the work" implies "I don't get any support." Where "All I ask is ten minutes of your time" says, in effect: "We never see each other these days. We've become like two trains passing in the night."

Should these brief examples sound familiar, husbands and wives might re-examine their continuing battles over roles . . . and the motivation behind those battles.

In such discussions, couples might question: Are we discussing problems around making beds instead of problems around making love? Are we focusing on socks rather than focusing on support? Are we saying "All I want is ten minutes" because of something lacking in the other twenty-three hours and fifty minutes in our day?

Here again, as long as a couple's significant problems remain obscured by insignificant arguments, their ensuing anger over minor issues continues to be distorted and derailing, as well as difficult to understand. (Let alone impossible to resolve.)

The case of a three-peckered goat

Let us take a common example where sexual roles were not discussed in a seven-year marriage. Instead, there were frequent arguments between husband and wife (Mr. and Mrs. J) over nonsexual duties, like who fixes the sink and who is responsible for putting the children to bed? And when?

In this case, the husband described their battles during a session in marital therapy. He said:

"After a five-day business trip, I drive home from the airport horny as a three-peckered goat. Over the years, however, I've learned what to expect on opening the front door. First, my wife greets me with a list of projects: 'The sink leaks' . . . 'The car battery's dead' . . . 'Lightbulbs need replacing' . . . (You name it, I fix it). Then, our kids are awake an hour past their normal bedtime 'waiting for Daddy.' Finally, when my wife and I do get into bed, she starts an argument over anything from the kids' bedtime to that kitchen sink. Instead of making love, we end up fighting."

It was at this point Mrs. J interrupted. As I earlier mentioned (see page 83) she told a different version of the same story.

"Whenever my husband returns from a business trip, he

comes home and wants to go directly to bed. With me. The problem is that I can't make love quickly on those nights. Rather than being in heat, like him, after four or five days apart I need more time to warm up and feel close before making love. I really want to talk over dinner . . . enjoy a bath together . . . be held in bed . . . I need to go slow. But my husband comes on like gangbusters. I guess that my greeting him with chores and children are my ways of slowing him down or saying 'no' on those nights after a trip."

Mr. J's initial reaction to his wife's "I need to go slow" was simply, "Why didn't you tell me?" On his part Mr. J readily agreed to spend more time with his wife before having sex. (Indeed, he saw the reality in her need, not for quickies, but for those cuddles, huddles, and holds.) On her part: Mrs. J vowed not to subject her husband to dead batteries or live children upon his opening the front door on those particular nights. Thus, with less anger between them, Mr. and Mrs. J began to define problems and offer solutions in the highly charged area of sexual roles for the first time in their seven-year marriage.

Beyond the Anger III: Small Changes Make Big Differences

Frequently, one partner's minor shift breaks a major log jam over roles. In the last case, "Go slower" before and during lovemaking represented a minor yet necessary change in the husband's role as lover. Necessary if he and his wife were to get beyond, not only Mrs. J's anger, but beyond Mr. J's "Me, Tarzan. You, Jane" approach to making love.

Of course, the simplest directions, like "Go slow," may be the hardest to put into practice. For example, those previous instructions, "Don't come on like gangbusters," required seven years for the wife to put into words. They also realistically required months for the husband and wife to put into effect. This reality of a couple's needing time to implement a "minor" change should not be forgotten. Nor should it negate the value of making small changes.

Let us now look at two nonsexual equivalents of "Don't come on like gangbusters." These include: (1) "Don't criticize me in public" and (2) "Don't expect *me* to handle *your* mother (or father)."

1. *"Don't criticize me in public": The role of critic.* As the helpful part of "Don't play Tarzan" are the instructions "Go slow"; so too, the positive side of "Don't be critical of me in front of other people" is "Support me." Thus, in public, no announcements: "If I've heard this story once . . . ," "Here we go again . . . ," "This is where I came in . . . " No interruptions: A husband's walking away from his wife in mid-sentence. A wife's turning to begin another conversation ten seconds before the punchline of her husband's story. An obvious yawn. A dirty look. A sarcastic laugh. No embarrassing revelations on secret subjects: From the wife's specifics: "Would you believe that he picks grey hairs out of his moustache with my tweezers?" To the husband's vague: "But you should see her in the morning." The simplest rule is: No displays, overt or covert, that tend to undermine the other person in public.

Support in public, however, means not only the absence of direct or indirect criticism, but also: An approving nod, smile, touch, or glance. An ability to laugh. An interest in listening with undivided attention. In short: A desire to please the person we love. Or, as one marriage counselor put it when asked the facetious question: "What do you think of a couple who listens to each other tell a joke in public, a story they've obviously heard a dozen times before, still, this couple laughs like crazy every time?!" Her reply was simply: "Either it's a hell of a joke, or it's a hell of a couple."

(See also "Praise: The Minimum Daily Requirement," page

20; "Conversations in Public," page 8; and "Concern—Kill 'em in Private," page 33.)

2. *"Don't expect me to handle your mother": The role of married sons and daughters.* Most newly-wed couples hope for good relations with their in-laws. And vice versa. Yet mother-in-law jokes aside, problems do arise between generations—daughters and new mothers, sons and new fathers (or any combination thereof). Unfortunately, in some families, the ensuing tensions go on . . . and on . . . and on.

Should misunderstandings or resentments build up between generations, one helpful solution involves the husband dealing with his parents, the wife with hers. From the couple's perspective, the following "identified problems" are not untypical. On the other hand, the "suggested solutions" might appear too simple to be real or too good to be true.

From the daughter-in-law's viewpoint:

Complaint 1:	*Your mother always brings bakery goods when she knows I prefer to do my own baking. Hints don't help.*
Son's role and potential solution:	I'll do more than hint. I'll tell her "No more food" when she visits.
Complaint 2:	*Do you realize that your mom still addresses letters to us in your name only?*
Son's role:	I never noticed. That's ridiculous—we've been married four years. I'll remind her.
Complaint 3:	*I try hard to please your mother during her visits. But she's never complimented me . . . on the house, the kids, the meals, on you . . . nothing!*
Son's role:	Now you see why I'm so lousy at giving compliments. Anyway, maybe you shouldn't try so hard. Just know: It's her problem, not your's.
Complaint 4:	*Your father helps us a lot. But there's a price to pay. He tries to run our lives.*

Son's role:	Look, he's been doing it with me for thirty years. And he's not going to change with us. So let's cut down on his gifts and visits. I'll be the one to say "no."

From the son-in-law's viewpoint:

Complaint 1:	*When your father begins telling one of his stories—don't just get up from the table and leave me.*
Daughter's role and potential solution:	You're right. I can tell Daddy when he's boring us much easier than you can.
Complaint 2:	*Whenever we visit your parents, I feel neglected after the first few days.*
Daughter's role:	We're together all year—you big baby. But it's not my folks' fault. It's mine. Next time, I'll try not to forget you.
Complaint 3:	*Should your mom and dad visit us, they sit around the living room for days. They drive me crazy.*
Daughter's role:	Okay. From now on, I'll do a better job of scheduling outside activities during their visits.
Complaint 4:	*How can I tell your mother to stop lecturing us about security and our future?*
Daughter's role:	You could . . . but I will.

Here again, the purpose in clarification of roles is to minimize arguments. To reduce minor (that frequently become "major") irritants by minimal changes on the couple's part. Husband and wife take action with their respective parents (even if it's to say, "My father won't change. But we can readjust our expectations of him").

As a result: Beyond the anger with mothers- or fathers-in-law lies not only a better relationship with them, but eventually, a better line of communication among all members of the family.

Beyond the Anger IV:
Ultimate Goals

Do I mean that two lovers should define and divide every function around the house? Must they set up fixed guidelines from
which there is no escape? Must they become so rigid about all
duties that nothing is left to chance?

Not really.

Indeed, the point is not whether we follow house rule "A":
See what needs to be done—and do it. Or, rule "B": Let's decide
—who is responsible? The point is that regardless of style, we
must get beyond arguments over who picks up socks or children,
who handles money or mothers-in-law.

Our goal should be to create as non-angry an atmosphere at
home as possible. A climate in which our time and energy is
not bound up in daily squabbles over routine chores. But rather,
it is available to deal with the more complicated roles in both
our public and private lives: Marital roles, parental roles, career
roles, sexual roles. Roles where, in fact, energy is necessary and
time required, if we are to help each other resolve the larger
problems facing us in our relationship.

Goals I: Help
With Major Roles

Husbands and wives are the logical people to help one another
clarify their major roles in life. They do so before marriage;
why not do so after it?

During a couple's courtship, hours upon hours are filled
with discussions of future plans: How to live? What to do?
Where to travel? With children or without them? Before marriage, afternoons and evenings are consumed with talk of "I

want to have your baby." . . . "No babies. Let's wait at least
five years." . . . "I hate my work." . . . "I love mine." . . . "Let's
take six months off from both our jobs to travel." . . . and on into
the night.

Whereas, in such cases, two lovers may see life as it should
be—not as it will be—what is the difference? Talk of future
hopes adds excitement to their lives. Dreams fuel their love
affair with energy and expectations. No matter how real or
unreal those expectations, possibilities seem unlimited: "Do
what you want, darling. If you're happy . . . I'm happy." "After
school, we can move anywhere in the country." "After this job,
we'll have money to see Europe." "After this year . . ."

After marriage, however, something changes.

Our daily realities and routines chip away at these hours of
delightful discussion. Problems over minor functions begin to
obscure questions about major roles. Rather than discuss "How
to live?" we begin to focus on "How to survive?" Dead batteries,
dirty socks, leaking sinks, dinner dishes, demanding kids, and
visiting in-laws begin to monopolize our time and conversation.

Yet, our preoccupation with daily survival doesn't negate
the basic fact: If discussion of basic roles proved helpful before
marriage, it proves doubly helpful after marriage. In truth, such
questions as: What to do? How to live? Where to move?
(luxuries in our premarital days) become *necessities* in our
marital years.

For example, let us briefly examine several basic dilemmas for
today's woman: In a good relationship, how can husband and
wife not continue to question: Do we want children? And if
the answer is "no," what career, job, activity, or service can bring
a sense of fulfillment? If the answer is "yes," or if there are
already children, how much time to spend with them? How to
find outside stimulation? (Several hours per week . . . per day
. . . on a full-time basis?) And if there is to be a full-time career
for the mother: Are not a few good hours with her children
better than many bad ones? Or, if the woman is to be a full-

time parent: What lies beyond her role as mother and wife? Especially when the children enter school or leave home, how does she transfer her energies from house to outside world? What are her fears in that transition? Indeed, what are her husband's?

What about the husband? Premarital questions such as "What to do?" and "Where to live?" also become practical problems for him in life after marriage.

In such or similar decisions, I think, wives can prove invaluable to their man. Because his "right" answers stem from the right questions (as is also true for the wife), she can start by helping the husband raise key questions, such as: Why move? What are the new (or old) job's rewards beside money? What are the alternatives? Looking ahead ten years at work, where are the heroes? If they do exist—what price success? If they don't exist—why stay with the job, firm, organization, or institution? More directly related to the wife: What lies beyond the husband's role at work? How might he improve his other roles: As a husband? A father? A lover? From where come the hours? From where the energy? How might the wife help him to put more time and interest into the family? Wherein lies his reluctance? Wherein lies hers?

We need time: we need each other

Should quick answers exist for these questions, I do not know them. As there are no magic solutions for the wife's problem: "Beyond the family how do I achieve a sense of fulfillment?" So too, there are no overnight answers for the man's plight: "I see no heroes ten years ahead of me, but what are my alternatives?" Indeed, between raising such questions and resolving them, couples need to talk for weeks . . . months . . . years.*

* Talking, of course, is the process. And here many couples would argue that it's the process that matters not the goal; the journey, not the arrival.

Although seemingly simple and prosaic, these dilemmas about major roles are complex and continuing ones. Continuing, because answers before marriage change after it. Decisions last year may not apply this year. Answers last month not fit next month. Thus, meaningful solutions can only follow a couple's ongoing discussions with the person most directly involved with their problems: Each other. As was true in their premarital relationship, I think two lovers are the logical people to help raise and resolve these highly individual questions. Not only does a husband know his wife best. But also, her decisions affect him most, and vice versa.

My feeling is that struggling with basic roles, we need our partner's help. Pressured to talk about changes at work or home, we need someone to listen. Feeling anxious about future plans, we need someone to absorb our anxiety rather than contribute to it with his own fears, misgivings, trepidations, and tensions. Needing support, we want encouragement during periods of crisis. Feeling "down," we need our loved-one to lift us up and share our problems—as well as be helpful with them.

To succeed, however, our up/down relationship must function like a balanced seesaw. As listener, we must feel that our turn to be heard will come later. We must know that our partner will also be "up" for us in the future. That he will absorb our tensions. That he will offer help and encouragement with the more crucial roles in our life—be they in our career-life, home-life, or sex-life.

Goals II: Flexibility
With More Roles

Realistically, however, we often lack this ability to reverse roles in marriage. Instead of talking and listening with equal facility, we become locked into fixed and familiar positions. We say, "He talks, I listen," or "I support him, but he has trouble supporting me," or "I soak up his anxiety, but he can't tolerate mine." In shorthand, we describe our complicated roles in terms of simplified polarities. We summarize:

He's reserved.	I'm spontaneous.
He's thoughtful.	I'm emotional.
He's serious.	I'm easy-going.
He's decisive.	I'm indecisive.
He's energetic.	I'm lazy.
He's tight.	I'm generous.
He's respectable.	I'm slightly crazy.
He's organized.	I'm scatter-brained.
He's angry.	I'm depressed.
	and the list goes on. . . .

Thus, over several years, we tend to get pigeon-holed as "the talker" or "listener," "organizer" or "scatter-brain," "martyr" or "tyrant" in the family. And this rigidity of roles and self-fulfilling prophesy, I think, leads to inevitable problems.

For example, the following complaints illustrate typical resentments which develop in one-sided relationships.

From a husband in a six-year marriage: "I guess you might call me the decision-maker at home. My wife's always been the quiet and shy type—even before we met. Usually, I don't mind her failure to initiate things with me. But when I'm saying 'Let's go out tonight' or 'Let's make love' ninety-nine percent of the time, it gets pretty old. After six years, it also gets damn boring."

More specifically, he added: "It's not like I'm asking her to seduce me every night. Just surprise me. Maybe once she could greet me after work with the news: A babysitter's coming and we're going out to dinner. Or, surprise me by putting her arm in mine on the way to a restaurant. Or, at home, cook a special dinner and add candlelight. The truth is that any small innovation on her part would be a step in the right direction."

From a wife in an eighteen-year marriage: "I'm both the martyr and mother to a husband and four kids. As for my husband, it's true that I enjoy caring for his needs during most of the year. Yet, should I become ill—God forbid—he gets furious at me or sick himself. At those moments, without any help when I'm down, I feel the impulse to call someone. But there's no one to call. So, I just become very depressed about no one ever mothering me."

Blaming herself, as was her style, the wife concluded: "It's probably my own fault for waiting the whole year, until I get sick, to have him take care of me. In fact, my needing support is probably like our needing sex. On a weekly basis. Not a yearly one. But how can you teach a man to mother his wife after eighteen years of not mothering her?"

Lastly, from an "explosive" husband in a new remarriage: "For some reason, I'm the person who gets mad and gives lectures in the family. Whenever my wife begins to get angry at me, I go wild as soon as she opens her mouth. It's an automatic response. Not only yelling and screaming. But, right or wrong—she's always wrong. It's ridiculous." Adding a footnote on his temper tantrums, the man said: "My rages are the single part of our relationship that haven't changed from day one. I don't even know where to begin."

One starting point is the realization that most couples become locked into fixed roles in some part of married life. These roles, in turn, often lead to complaints such as: A wife's lack of initiative "ninety-nine percent of the time." A man's inability to care for his wife even during an illness. A husband's intolerance to criticism and his subsequent failure to let his wife express her anger.

I think the first question is: Where in *our* particular relationship do imbalances exist? Do we see ourselves, at least in part, as the decision-maker, mother, martyr, quiet, angry, or predictable member of the family? And if so, does this stereotyped view prevent us from shifting roles when necessary to help the person we love?

Ideally, of course, we would have the capacity to move from

no initiative to some initiative; from predictability to spontaneity; from anger to support; from seriousness to foolishness. In an intimate relationship, not only must there be a time for every emotion under the sun. But there must also be an ability to express these emotions.

Or, to paraphrase Ecclesiastes: If there is a *time* to weep, so too, there must be an *ability* to weep, an ability to laugh; an ability to mourn, an ability to dance; an ability to embrace, an ability to be far from embraces; an ability to be silent, an ability to speak.

And this ability to move in opposite directions implies, I believe, flexibility of roles. A flexibility to give comfort as well as be comforted; to be decisive as well as to be dependent; to use the head as well as the heart. And during lovemaking: A flexibility to be aggressive or submissive; expressive or silent; gentle or strong; leisurely or quick; experimental or safe.

Sexually or nonsexually, if flexibility is our goal, I think we need not seek fifty-fifty balance in those one-sided areas of our relationship which cause problems. All we really need is some movement in the right direction. To move from no initiative to some initiative. From little spontaneity to more spontaneity.

However, "movement" implies change. So, let us in the final chapter, question: How might we change? In nonpsychological language, what framework might help us in the pursuit of new behavior?

9

Making Changes: Responsibility, Alternatives, and Courage

The complexities of how people change are not well understood. But clearly, the process is a difficult and hazardous one.

To change our behavior requires giving up safe habits, even when those habits have proved self-defeating to us in the past. It involves lowering established defenses, and our subsequent exposure and vulnerability to other people. Especially those closest to us who are familiar with our sensitivities and weaknesses. It means exploring unfamiliar territory, with no absolute guarantee of finding better ways to deal with previous problems. Hence, making changes is not only a risky business, but an unpredictable one.

As a psychiatrist friend once remarked: "After twenty years of seeing people who hope to change, I still can't predict who will or won't succeed in achieving his goals during psychotherapy. You never know."

Whereas I basically agree with that observation, I also believe that certain qualities are shared by people who develop new patterns of behavior. With or without benefit of psychotherapy, these qualities include: (1) A person's acceptance of responsibility for his current as well as future behavior, (2) His ability to see alternate ways of dealing with repetitious problems, and (3) His courage to try such alternatives.

Although this framework is an admittedly and deliberately simplified one—and obviously, not the full story—let us examine these three ingredients as they apply to shifts in a couple's relationship.

Responsibility I: A Daily Job

At work, the motto: "If you do something, do it well" is an acceptable avenue to success. A person's working hard "every day in every way" makes sense, if he hopes to master his job and enjoy its rewards. On the other hand: To let days or weeks pass without performing one's responsibilities is to insure frustration and failure.

Do not similar conditions exist at home?

I think so. My feeling is that we must pay attention to daily details, as much in private as in public. Ultimately, we must accept responsibility for our successful performance, at work or home, regardless of what our task is called. Be it: Insuring a fifteen-minute review each night; listening as well as speaking; offering praise; requesting privacy; enforcing such house rules as "We don't go to bed angry"; or letting our changing sexual needs be known to each other.

Regardless of how long-standing our habits, how deeply rooted our behavior, we must simply accept responsibility for our daily actions.* After all, if we aren't responsible for our success in everyday living, who is?

Responsibility II: "You, We, or Me?"

Responsibility for problems can be blamed on internal forces ("me") or external realities ("you," "they," and "it"). To admit

---

* I realize that some psychotherapists, feeling that all current behavior is overdetermined by past background (much of which is unconscious), would question how a person can be responsible for his unconscious actions.

inner causes, we must turn our eyeballs inward and look at our liver or conscience, laying at our own feet a large quantum of responsibility for specific difficulties. To blame external realities, of course, is much simpler. For example:

A high school girl loses a tennis match at school. Who is responsible?

"The kid who beat me had an aluminum racket."
or
"I didn't practice hard enough this month."

A lawyer has financial troubles with his partner. Who is responsible?

"The other attorney is a goddamn money-grubber."
or
"I have trouble discussing money with him . . . with my clients . . . with myself."

After three weeks, a couple wants to evict the husband's brother who's been staying in their apartment. Why the delay?

"He's never home to discuss the subject."
or
"We don't know how to tell him: 'Time's up. You're driving us crazy.' "

A working wife can't share her day with the husband:

"He has enough pressures."
or
"I fear his anger—or worse, indifference—should I complain about my job."

The four-year-old son of an engineer draws with indelible ink on a freshly painted wall. Why the destruction?

"Ben's angry and frustrated with his new baby sister."
or
"He needs limits, but I have trouble saying 'no' to him."

In all cases, both statements might be true. But it is our emphasis that counts. Passing the buck or finding scapegoats, we abdicate responsibility for our behavior. And thereby, we abdicate a large measure of control over that behavior. However, seeing our role in creating problems, we can do something about them. In part, at least, we're in charge here. Or, to paraphrase that familiar presidential quote: "The buck stops with me."

Responsibility III:
Learning From Mistakes

Aside from "I, I, I, me, me, me, my, my, my," couples hear plenty of "you, you, you" in most relationships. "You don't love me anymore . . ." "I hate it when you . . ." "The trouble with you is . . ." Paradoxically, such angry outbursts may give two people an opportunity to learn from their mistakes. How?

Obviously, it does not help to repeat the same global "You always . . ." month after month (year after year). It does help, I think, when couples accept responsibility for ending their accusations with specific suggestions as to how "you" might prevent arguments in the future.

Let's take fights which run in twenty-eight to thirty-day cycles: The man yells, "After six years, I still think it's my fault that you become moody and irrational each month. How do I know that it's your period?" He adds, "So, warn me the curse is coming and I won't take it so personally." Or, the wife ends the same fight with different instructions: "When you notice I'm jumpy or tense, don't just scream at me: 'You're tense, YOU'RE TENSE!!' Wait a few minutes, ask what's wrong, even if I say 'nothing,' insist we talk. But don't withdraw and let several days pass."

As I have stressed throughout the book: From monthly blues to daily clashes, *relationships grow when two people teach each other about their needs.* In essence, one person must say, "When

I'm upset, here's what you can do about it." And the second person must try to change his behavior accordingly. It always takes two. One is as responsible for learning from his mistakes as is the other for teaching him about them.

But, here, some readers may understandably object to being responsible for accommodating to their partner's needs. They view marital accommodation and personal growth as mutually exclusive. Or, to put it another way, they may see the problem in "either/or" terms. *Either* I accommodate to my spouse, *or* I preserve my own individuality. Hence, accommodation becomes synonymous with loss of self or identity.

Rather than an either/or viewpoint, however, I would suggest that "both/and" are necessary. Two people must both be responsible for accommodation at home, and, at the same time, be responsible for their own growth and development. Indeed, growth of the individual seems to me a basic prerequisite for the growth of any relationship. Needless to add, there are times when a husband or wife's development clearly threatens the relationship's development, or vice versa. At such times, I think, it requires an enormous amount of work, not only to define the problem, but to attempt various solutions.

Again, it may sound exhausting. It is exhausting. Yet, I know of no short cut to this kind of individual responsibility for *both* personal *and* collective change within a marriage.

(Responsibility for identifying problems and suggesting solutions was also previously discussed under "Asking for Support," page 25; "Taking a Stand," page 42; and "Talking and Doing: The Key to Changing Roles," page 127.)

Responsibility IV: "I Can't
Change . . . That's the Way I Am!"

Why do some couples fail to learn from their mistakes?

One reason lies in the fact that husbands and wives frequently reach an impasse when one partner shouts: "I can't change . . . that's the way I am." Or, he says:

"If you don't like it . . . "
"That's me. I can't help it."
"Goddammit. I'm sorry. But I'm doing the best I can . . . "

Similar expressions tend to punctuate a couple's fights over everything from spending money to handling children, cleaning house to making love.

The difficulty is that such punctuation points are not merely commas or semicolons in the midst of battle. They are periods. End of discussion. No more. "I've had it." There's nothing left to say. "I can't change—that's me." And, in these situations, what can the other person say?

"That's not you?"
     or
"You're not doing the best you can?"

Such retorts only lead to the "Yes, I am . . . No, you're not" kind of dead ends that prevent resolution of anger and arguments. For example, let us review an impasse over making love, and combine several previous points about sexual signals, complaints, and practice.

If we want to criticize our partner about his silence in bed, we might comment:

"I wish you'd say more during lovemaking."
"Anything but silence."
"Say what you'd like me to do."
"Moaning louder or thrusting harder before your climax would help me to come with you."

Hearing such reactions, as I mentioned in Chapter 5, our partner may think not only "Something's missing in bed" but also "Something's missing in me." And, drawing such conclusions, he's likely to respond with a mixture of anger, embarrassment, and insecurity. A combination of feelings which often culminate (silently or aloud) in the defensive reaction: "Love me (the way I am) or leave me." Or, "Dammit, if you don't like it . . ." Period. End of comment on sexual signals.

At this point, I think that we have two basic choices: If taken literally, we must accept "I'm sorry. That's the way I am," as an end to further discussion. An abdication of our partner's responsibility for new behavior. Change is impossible. If taken figuratively, however, we need not accept such comments at face value. Indeed, I believe that we must be responsible for hearing "I can't change," not as a non-negotiable demand and definitive statement, but as a *defensive* statement. And we should proceed accordingly.

Knowing that criticism hurts, we should recognize the hurt and not open deeper wounds. Here, too, we can pick a later time to discuss the subject of new behavior. (See "Sexual Complaints," page 83.) A time when our partner feels receptive instead of defensive, relaxed instead of tense, close rather than distant. In the case of bedroom silence, a time when our lover can discuss sexual signals, in spite of his initial resistance to them. A time he can say:

> "How do I suddenly begin talking or moaning in bed without feeling ridiculous?"
> "I'd feel phony."
> "It would come out all wrong."
> "You'd think I'd gone crackers."
> "*I'd* think I'd gone crackers."
> "I'm afraid that you'd laugh at me."

With these words, however, our husband or wife's message is not "I can't change" but "I'm afraid to change." A difference which explains, at least in part, that initial defensiveness; and which tends to stimulate further discussion rather than stifle it. The crucial difference is that our lover is again responsible for his behavior. With the result: Change is again possible.

Responsibility V:
"Yield," "Slow," and "Stop"

One final thought about responsibility in repetitious fights: It helps when two people accept responsibility for retracing their habitual human collisions back to identifiable intersections. At those prior crossroads, marked in retrospect by familiar signposts, couples might learn where and when in future crises to "yield," "slow," or "stop" and minimize predictable damages.*

In Chapter 3, I mentioned Friday night exhaustion as one signal of impending disaster. Under "Fatigue: The Universal Allergy," various detours were offered for exhausted couples who hoped to avoid a collision course by week's end. Anger, itself, was discussed as another helpful indicator of the distance between couples. Frequent or intense arguments being one indication to slow down and make time for each other.

In Chapter 5, I observed that sexual boredom, like anger, may also represent a signal for more closeness in an intimate relationship. Escape and erotic fantasies possibly serving as the tip of a sexual iceberg. "I'm feeling trapped" or "I'm fantasizing more" being potential warning signs of what isn't happening at home. Or, at least, what isn't happening in bed.

At this point, let us ask: How might couples identify their own warning signals? Ones which might prove helpful in repetitious crises?

Husband and wife can start by reviewing the internal as well as external events which culminate in predictable problems. A couple's responsibility is several fold: (1) To retrace their explosions back to obvious crossroads where they might have turned left instead of right (or vice versa), (2) to recognize these cross-

---

* I am reminded of Noel Coward's *Private Lives* in which a honeymoon couple makes the following pact: If they are about to fight, one of them will shout the warning, "Solomon Isaacs"—and both will keep silent for two minutes.

roads in the future, and (3) once reached in the future, both partners must accept responsibility for trying to move in new directions.

One of the most familiar, least recognized, warnings before a predictable collision was discovered by a carpenter and his wife in marital therapy. The following dialogue is an abbreviated version of that discovery:

Wife: Everything's okay now. We're not having any problems.

Husband: No problems. It's simply that we're not talking at night.

Wife: But we talked last week and there haven't been any problems since then . . .

Husband: There will be in a few weeks.

Wife: What do you mean?

Husband: You'll suddenly realize that I've been withdrawn for about a month. Then, you'll get very tense. And we'll have a big scene about your not feeling loved.

Wife: What are you saying?

Husband: That it's much easier for us to read or watch television than to make conversation. And, that our *not talking* causes me to veer away and begin withdrawing from you. If there is a crossroad, that's an early one. The problem is that you don't notice until we're a million miles apart.

Wife: Maybe you're right. So, why don't you just say "let's talk?"

Husband: Because there's a lazy part of me that doesn't want to talk.

Wife: You talk in this office.

Husband: Here, it's an expectation. Besides, at thirty dollars an hour, we have to—talk's not cheap.

Therapist: How might it become an expectation at home?

Wife: He could force me to put down my book or turn off the T.V. He could say: "Time to talk."

Husband: Sure, but you could help. You could see that we have a drink before dinner to get us into a relaxed mood. You could insure that we eat in privacy, without the kids, two or three times a week. If we're alone at supper, our talking might become more of an expectation.

Wife: Okay. I'll accept responsibility for our eating without the children several times a week. Let's start there and see what happens.

In this family, as others, I think that it's easier to notice everyday signals (such as: "We should turn off the damn television," "Stop reading," "We should talk") than it is to act upon such signals and move in new directions. Yet, our seeing these choices, at the time, is a vital step. Vital because we catch a glimpse of paths not previously taken. Of alternate routes. Of points at which we might change directions . . . and change behavior. For, as Allen Wheelis has succinctly concluded:*

"If . . . the greater awareness is of options unnoticed, of choices denied, of other ways to live, then freedom will be increased and with it greater responsibility for what we have been, are, and will be."

Because I so strongly believe in this principle, the next five sections are devoted to the problem of seeing choices in making changes.

* Allen Wheelis, "How People Change" first appeared in *Commentary*, May 1969. Portions of the essay also appeared in *The Desert* (New York, Basic Books, 1970) and in slightly different form in *How People Change* (New York, Harper & Row, 1973).

Alternatives I:
On the Ropes. In a Corner

Here, let us draw another analogy. This time, to prizefighting: A boxer is free to jab, hook, move left or right, punch or counterpunch, as long as he fights in the middle of the ring. Should that fighter be maneuvered into a corner, however, not only will he be trapped, but his alternatives are severely limited. Defensively, he can cover up, grab, or hold on. Offensively, he can move in one direction, straight ahead. Only after the boxer punches his way back toward the ring's center is he again free to move in all directions. Thus, one job of a prizefighter is to avoid being backed into corners.

So, too, I think, many of us get trapped in the corners of daily living. When we feel "boxed-in" by circumstances, our alternatives also disappear. Under pressure, we frequently see only one or two directions in which to escape from our predicament. We say, "But I have no choice in the matter. What else can I do?"

The first thing to do is recognize the corners we create for ourselves. Our self-made ropes that limit freedom of action. What follows, here, are descriptions of several common ways we think (or don't think) about alternatives. Ways, in turn, which tend to restrict the choices available to us.

Alternatives II:
From "A" to "Z"

The either/or syndrome

In many situations, our limited view of a problem is commonly prefaced by the words: "Either/or." *Either* I choose "A" *or* I'm left with "Z." Either/or becomes synonymous with alternatives. For example:

A sixty-year-old corporation executive thinks about divorcing his wife after thirty-five years of marriage. Involved with his former secretary, the man views his future in two dimensions:

Either: I return home to my wife and same old problems.

Or: I marry this young girl (she's only twenty-four!), even though her three small kids are younger than my grandchildren.

A forty-five-year-old attractive widow complains of depression. In talking about problems, she mentions that her nonexistent social life reflects an inner bind. She thinks:

Either: My friends introduce me to respectable, educated, and eligible men. Which, if I'm lucky, happens twice a year.

Or: I start frequenting bars—which just isn't my style.

A twenty-one-year-old girl, recently married, feels bored at work and home. She desperately wants "something to happen" that might change her life. Two paths seem open:

Either: I continue as a waitress—the world's most boring job.

Or: I get pregnant and have a baby—which we really can't afford for at least three more years.

The middle ground

Whereas *either/or* thinking does offer two solutions to most problems, such "A" to "Z" answers overlook the middle ground between "B" and "Y." Maneuvering ourselves into psychological corners, we remain blind to other choices. For example: That widow's either "proper introductions to men," or "picking them up in bars" neglects a vast range of alternate ways to meet men, such as: (b) evening classes, (c) weekend retreats, (d) volunteer work, (e) political activity, (f) computer dating, (g) vacations, (h) church groups, (i) a new job, (j) an expanded circle of friends, (k) . . .

Either "the old problems with my wife" or "new ones with my mistress" neglects the corporate executive's other options. He might also consider: (b) separation without immediate divorce or remarriage, (c) no final decision for six months, (d) marital counseling, (e) individual psychotherapy, (f) living with his secretary and her three kids for a trial period, (g) . . .

Many problems, of course, are easier to view in two-dimensional terms. As that secretary said, when her male friend eventually recommended they seek premarital counseling: "Are you kidding? The problem is . . . to marry or not to marry? I don't want some psychiatrist opening the lid on more trouble and confusing things."

Such sentiments, I think, accurately reflect a common paradox. Many men and women under stress in some corner of daily living will translate "more alternatives" into "more pressure." These people may understand choices "A" or "Z" and see their way clearly in those two directions. But they are overwhelmed, or frightened, at the prospect of figuring out alternatives B, C, D . . . X, or Y. As the secretary tells her lover in effect: "Look. I know how I feel, don't confuse me with the facts."

Predicting the consequences

Not only must we notice our "either/or" thinking, but it also helps to predict the consequences. For example: Should that eligible widow hope to alter her life by finding a respectable man, her future actions, in large measure, depend upon her current plans. She weighed two options: Either proper introductions to men or picking them up in bars. Yet, with these either/or choices, does she not move herself from one corner into another? Do not her two alternatives more-often-than-not lead to the predictable consequences of further isolation, loneliness, and depression?

Or, that business executive's dilemma: Either the "old problems with my wife" or "new ones with my mistress." Do not his "old problems" versus "new ones" become a springboard to continuing chaos and confusion in his private life? Would not his future problems be one result of his present alternatives?

Consequently, should the businessman anticipate chaos or the widow predict depression, both can scrap their blueprints and return to their respective drawing boards. They can explore the middle ground and make other plans. They can elect not to build their behavior on such obviously faulty foundations.

Another example illustrates this principle in more detail:

Mrs. T, a recently divorced nurse, wanted to change jobs in order to meet new people. Her initial offer was a sixty-hour per week faculty position in a local school of nursing. The job represented higher prestige, but at lower wages than her current job. Meaning that Mrs. T would have to moonlight nights or weekends in order to pay her bills. Anxious to change, however, she was relatively blind to the personal consequences of double-duty nursing. She thought: "Either I'm stuck in my same old rut for another ten years," or "I make compromises and work long hours." Fortunately, she discussed the offer before accepting it.

A friend asked bluntly: "How can you meet new people by working eight days a week? Sounds stupid to me." It also sounded crazy to her. Declining the job, Mrs. T admitted to herself that she felt pressured into a decision between two bad choices. Feeling cornered, she decided to put more irons into the professional fires of academic nursing. Finally, six months later, she found an eight-to-five teaching position ten months a year with commensurate salary. Between jobs, she was able to take a European vacation for the first time in her life. And, although she didn't meet "the" man in her travels, she had successfully remained out of a corner and free to move in various directions, privately and professionally.

Mrs. T's goal of meeting new people was enhanced by seeing alternatives (or lack of them), weighing consequences, finding new options, and ultimately choosing a suitable working blueprint on which to build her next few years.

In marriage, I believe that one of the most helpful services couples can render is to point out one another's either/or thinking. When we hear our partner speaking in "all or none" terms, it is often easier for us, the listener, to recognize that our spouse feels cornered, and that he needs help in seeing alternatives. Thus, if we hear our husband or wife saying: "It's either 'A' or 'Z,' " we can help by asking: "What about the middle ground of 'L, S, M, F, and T?' And equally important: What are the consequences of each?"

Alternatives III:
Actions Versus Reactions

Another self-made corner can be defined in terms of actions and reactions. Reactions are not unlike the counterpunch in boxing. One person lets another set the pace and act before he reacts to the situation. His daily moves are really countermoves. His seeming "actions" are truly reactions in disguise. His behavior, in large part, is therefore dictated by other people and outside events. The following thoughts were expressed by a seventeen-year-old adolescent, who recognized this punch-counterpunch way of living. He said:

"I react to everyone in my life. I'm like a chameleon, changing colors depending upon the people I'm around. For instance, should my friends want to cut fifth and sixth periods at school, I cut class with them. Should my dad hassle me about grades, I react and we end up in huge fights over dinner. When my girl friend wanted sex one night, with no contraceptives around, I gave in to her.

"Yet, I don't honestly like to cut classes each day or fight at home every night. And obviously, I didn't want that girl to become pregnant. But she did."

For this young man, "reactive" means created unwanted ends. "Let's cut fifth and sixth periods" led to poor grades which, in turn, increased the boy's anxiety about college. His father's "let's fight" (over those same grades) became the punch for his son's counterpunches over supper. "Let's make love" was the first step in an aborted pregnancy, which caused two young people and their families an enormous amount of pain.

Blind to his alternatives (for example, saying "no" to his father and friends—male and female), this high school senior saw himself the victim of his own reactions. From lower grades to an unwanted pregnancy, he felt trapped by "circumstances." He kept saying, "This isn't what I had in mind at all." And finally, "I have no control over these situations."

Such action/reaction patterns are extremely common in intimate relationships. From time to time, most of us feel immobilized or victimized by our reactions to a partner. Yet, in marriage, should we find ourselves constantly reacting to situations in self-defeating ways, it helps to ask: "What alternate *actions* are possible?" Put another way: To view our unhelpful reactions as crossroads where we have a choice of turning left instead of right, of going in reverse instead of proceeding straight ahead on a collision course.

Why is this recognition of crossroads and pathways so crucial—at the time, or even in retrospect? Simply because we cannot act upon our alternatives, unless we see them. Be the alternatives called paths not taken, options unnoticed, choices denied, or other ways to live.

A familiar example for many of us includes the following abbreviated sequence: Partner A is preoccupied for several days (or weeks) and Partner B *reacts* to the growing distance between them. Feeling neglected, B becomes equally distant and withdrawn. Later, when A finally notices B's coolness, A reacts in anger: "Goddammit, what in the hell's wrong with you now?" (Of course, A's rage only serves to confirm B's feelings of rejection and worthlessness.) In many relationships, A's anger produces a louder silence from B, who may soon find himself/herself screaming at the children or yelling at the dog. Indeed, B may notice an "over-reaction" to everyone.

In this case, A's action of being preoccupied is followed by B's reactions of (1) silence, (2) hurt, (3) coolness or tears, (4) anger at A's anger, (5) indignation at A's indifference, and (6) lashing out at innocent bystanders. Such cycles tend to end with A and B's (7) huge battles, and maybe, (8) good lovemaking.

During a cold war, however, A and B may not be aware of steps 2 (silence) through 7 (the "inevitable" argument). At the time, they may simply feel trapped by circumstances. Like that seventeen-year-old boy, they may think: "What's happening? I have no control over the situation." Partner B may notice A's growing preoccupation at home, but see no alternatives. B thinks "What can I do?" And, feeling hopeless, B chooses to do nothing about A's initial withdrawal. B reacts with silence. One reaction leads to another . . . and suddenly, it's at the point, "I have no choice in the matter."

Yet, there are other choices.

B might actively discuss A's preoccupation, instead of only feeling threatened or hurt by it. B might directly tell A that he's neglecting her (or vice versa), rather than indirectly feeling martyred or indignant. Hard as it may be at the time, B might use the reaction of silence as a signal to confront the problem. Thereby, B short-circuits (or speeds-up) a predictable chain of painful events (silence, hurt, anger, and so forth) that unquestionably result when two lovers' coolness toward each other lasts for several days or weeks.

But here, let us ask: Doesn't the nature of A's preoccupations influence B's reactions? For example: If A is concerned with a major exploratory operation . . . or with the fact that he's putting on too much weight . . . wouldn't it make a difference? If A is preoccupied with a failing business . . . or an improperly strung tennis racket . . . wouldn't it make a difference in B's interventions?

The answer, I think, is "yes" and "no."

On the one hand: Major problems such as exploratory surgery tend to be openly identified as the source of one's preoccupations. With an upcoming date in the hospital, A's worries are obvious and "legitimate." As are B's reactions of concern, sympathy, and understanding. B is also likely to know about the problem and not take it personally. Whereas, A's preoccupations over minor traumas such as weight, diet, or tennis, are often viewed by both partners as less legitimate. These worries are commonly embarrassing to A because he or she is preoccupied with something "so small." Consequently, A is less likely to share concerns. With the result: (1) B doesn't understand A's silence and tends to take it personally—often withdrawing from the situation, or (2) B guesses at A's preoccupations over "trivia" and is unsympathetic to the problem.

On the other hand: Sympathetic or not, I believe that B can abort a prolonged silence *by getting A to discuss the nature of the silent concern,* be it over a major crisis or minor irritant. Why? Because as I said earlier under a fifteen-minute review at night: When we share the little intimate details of our daily preoccupations, such preoccupations tend to intrude less between us at night. After we unwind, it is easier for us to listen. In squeezing our inner sponge, we not only relax but we are again ready to be refilled—alone or together. And the resulting climate at home is more favorable for better listening and better conversation.

Alternatives IV: Active or Passive;
a Choice Is a Choice Is a Choice

Many of us see ourselves in A and B's reactions to each other during a cold war, nod our head, say "true, true," and then react with silence the next time our partner withdraws from us. We don't really feel like thinking about crossroads and choices in the midst of battle. Besides, it's much easier to do nothing and wait for an apology.

However, it's helpful to recognize that our decision *to do nothing is a choice.* To "let it be" is one alternative.

Whereas our doing "nothing" is a passive alternative, it frequently carries the active hope that "something will happen to get me out of the predicament." During periods of coolness, for instance, we hope the other person will close the distance between us. "My wife will apologize," ending the silence. "My husband will come over and hold me," preventing the tears. Meanwhile, of course, we remain quietly wounded or not-so-quietly furious.

The important point, I believe, is not that we become passive in difficult situations, but how we arrive at that passivity. For example: In an argument, should we become silent and feel:

"I have no choice in the matter."
"What's happening?"
"I feel trapped."
"I need to escape."
"What can I do?"

The situation controls us. Any change hinges upon outside events and other people rescuing us from our plight.

On the other hand: Should we view our withdrawal as one of several alternatives and think, in effect: "I could break the silence, but I don't want to. At least, not now. . . ." We're responsible for our decisions and actions . . . including the choice to be passive. Here, the situation no longer controls us. Indeed, we have some control over it. And that, I believe, is a crucial difference.

Alternatives V:
Conclusions

Again, to quote Wheelis:*

"The place of insight is to illumine: To ascertain where one is, how one got there, how now to proceed, and to what end. It is a blueprint, as in building a house and may be essential, but no one achieves a house by blueprints alone, no matter how accurate or detailed. A time comes when one must take up hammer and nails."

Responsibility and alternatives aside, changes in people result from changes in their behavior. It is clear that a fat person cannot become thin without losing weight; any more than an alcoholic can rehabilitate himself without giving up liquor. As man does not live by bread alone, so too, people do not change by words alone.

None of us really develop new patterns of behavior by thinking or talking about a new course of action. We change by doing something about it. Ultimately, our deeds are what count; it is our performance that matters.

In an intimate relationship, we always reach that moment of truth when we must act in a situation. A moment when neither "alternatives" nor "responsibility" are enough to resolve our difficulties. At that point, we start to change—the hammer and nails part—by actually saying "Let's talk" or "I apologize" to end an argument; "I love you" in offering praise, "I'd like you to . . ." verbally or nonverbally, in expressing a sexual wish or need. And these changes, large or small, ultimately require not only trial and error, awkwardness and embarrassment, pa-

---

* Allen Wheelis, "How People Change," see footnote on page 155.

tience and practice, over years. But they require, I think, an
act of courage.

Change: An Act of Courage

> *Courage:* The response of facing and dealing with anything
> recognized as dangerous, difficult, or painful instead of
> withdrawing from it.
>
> —WEBSTER'S DICTIONARY

Most of us equate courage with crises in life. Our response to
an illness or death in the family. Our courage in leaving home
after fifteen years of a bad marriage. Our wife, during a twenty-
four-hour labor and difficult childbirth. Our husband saying
"no" to a secure job because of convictions about remaining his
own man.

In retrospect, such courageous acts under stress, these moments of truth, occur maybe half a dozen times in a lifetime
and are familiar to all of us. These moments are clear. We
either rise or fall, succeed or fail, in these once-in-a-decade kind
of tests. Yet, is courage always so dramatic?

My own feeling is that we face "difficult or painful" situations in which we must "deal or withdraw" not several times a
decade, but several times each day.

For example: Who amongst us hasn't faced a daily battery of
rationalizations around a regular schedule of physical exercise?
Rationalizations why we can't possibly spare that extra ten to
fifteen minutes a day necessary for Isometrics or Aerobics, twenty
pushups or thirty situps, a mile walk or jog. Or, in questions
of diet as well as exercise: Who amongst us (at some point in his
life) hasn't faced a daily struggle related to food and weight?
To eat or not to eat: A piece of buttered toast with breakfast?
A beer with lunch? Baked potato or dessert with dinner? Another cocktail? An extra glass of wine? As dieters or drinkers trying to break bad habits, do we not agonize and debate the pros

and cons of "just one more" at frequent intervals throughout the day?

And, at those moments, does it not require a small act of courage to break an old habit? Let alone, to develop a new one? At such times, we may know the "right" path. But we also recognize ourselves in Stephen Crane's lines about "the wayfarer" who

> Perceiving the pathway to truth,
> Was struck with astonishment.
> It was thickly grown with weeds.
> "Ha," he said,
> "I see that none has passed here
> In a long time."
> Later he saw that each weed
> Was a singular knife.
> "Well," he mumbled at last,
> "Doubtless there are other roads."*

If we need acts of daily courage to keep our body healthy, do we not also face similar struggles in keeping our marriage healthy—the everyday equivalents of saying "yes" or "no" to those extra calories. Do not most of us at various points in our week face minor, yet fundamental, crossroads in the relationship? "To speak or not to speak?" To deal or withdraw from an interpersonal problem? To share or remain silent? Beyond obvious joys and sorrows, to express feelings or bury them? To say "let's talk" or "I'm sorry" rather than continue a cold war? To attack issues rather than personalities? To voice compliments or explain hurts instead of putting the lid on our emotions, positive and negative?

Courage between husband and wife, I think, requires continuing attention to such dilemmas. An ability *not* to let problems slide by either ignoring them or "putting off for tomorrow." Daily courage involves a person's taking those first small steps

* Stephen Crane, *Collected Poems* (New York, Alfred A. Knopf, 1930), page 92.

on the path he knows to be the right one. Although that road may seem endless, painful, or thickly grown with weeds. Finally, and again, daily courage—to set forth, in order to change behavior—involves our accepting the wisdom of a simple thought expressed almost 2,500 years ago. For it was the sixth century B.C. when Lao-tse observed that even "A journey of a thousand miles must begin with a single step."

From a certain point onward there is no longer any turning back. That is the point that must be reached.

—FRANZ KAFKA

Afterword

Let us end with my opening words of caution. As I stated, the book's focus is upon the inner world of two people who like each other (most of the time). Thus, one assumption throughout all sections is the existence of basic good will between partners. A good will which implies that each person is willing to try and change parts of his behavior in order to please the other person.

Yet, realistically, what about the reader whose partner says, "Come on, forget it. Will you stop all that nonsense about communicating better—don't bother me."? How does a person cope with a mate who is indifferent to such advice as: "Let's talk on a daily basis . . . let's try to be more understanding . . . let's try to be more supportive of each other . . ."? What about homes in which one partner wants to change and the other does not?

Frankly, I again know of no easy answers to these questions. But I think there are probably three basic courses of action upon the recognition of such an impasse. We can (1) do nothing and resign ourselves to the status quo, (2) realize that our mate is unable or unwilling to change at the time and concentrate upon our own growth and development, and/or (3) seek the help of an outside person, be he clergyman or family doctor, psychiatrist or psychologist, social worker or lay counselor.

"How to" books (such as this one) may appear to provide answers, but we must remember that the end of *any* book is only the beginning. A springboard for a couple's discussion of their own specific problems. A vehicle for each pair to decide which ideas do and don't make sense; those guidelines which should or shouldn't be translated into action.

Depending upon the couple, some answers will be inappropriate and inapplicable. Other solutions, hopefully, will be amenable to modification, so as to meet specific difficulties in a particular relationship. While other solutions, I trust, will have direct application and offer immediate help at home. Let it suffice to say: A goal in all chapters of this book has been to present new as well as old ideas in as straightforward a manner as possible. Clear enough for a person to think "I agree" or "disagree." "You're right on" or "way off." Ultimately, of course, the for-better parts of marriage remain a highly individual matter.

One final note: A vital aspect of clarifying my thoughts has been the invaluable reactions of patients, students, friends, and family. I can only hope that such feedback will continue from readers. Of special interest would be the half-full rather than half-empty view of living together. The "what does work" side of married life which has not been mentioned in this book.

Your comments would be most appreciated and can be sent to me in care of the publisher: Harper & Row, 10 East 53rd St., New York, New York 10022.

Many thanks and good luck.